LITTLE
CROCHET
TREASURES

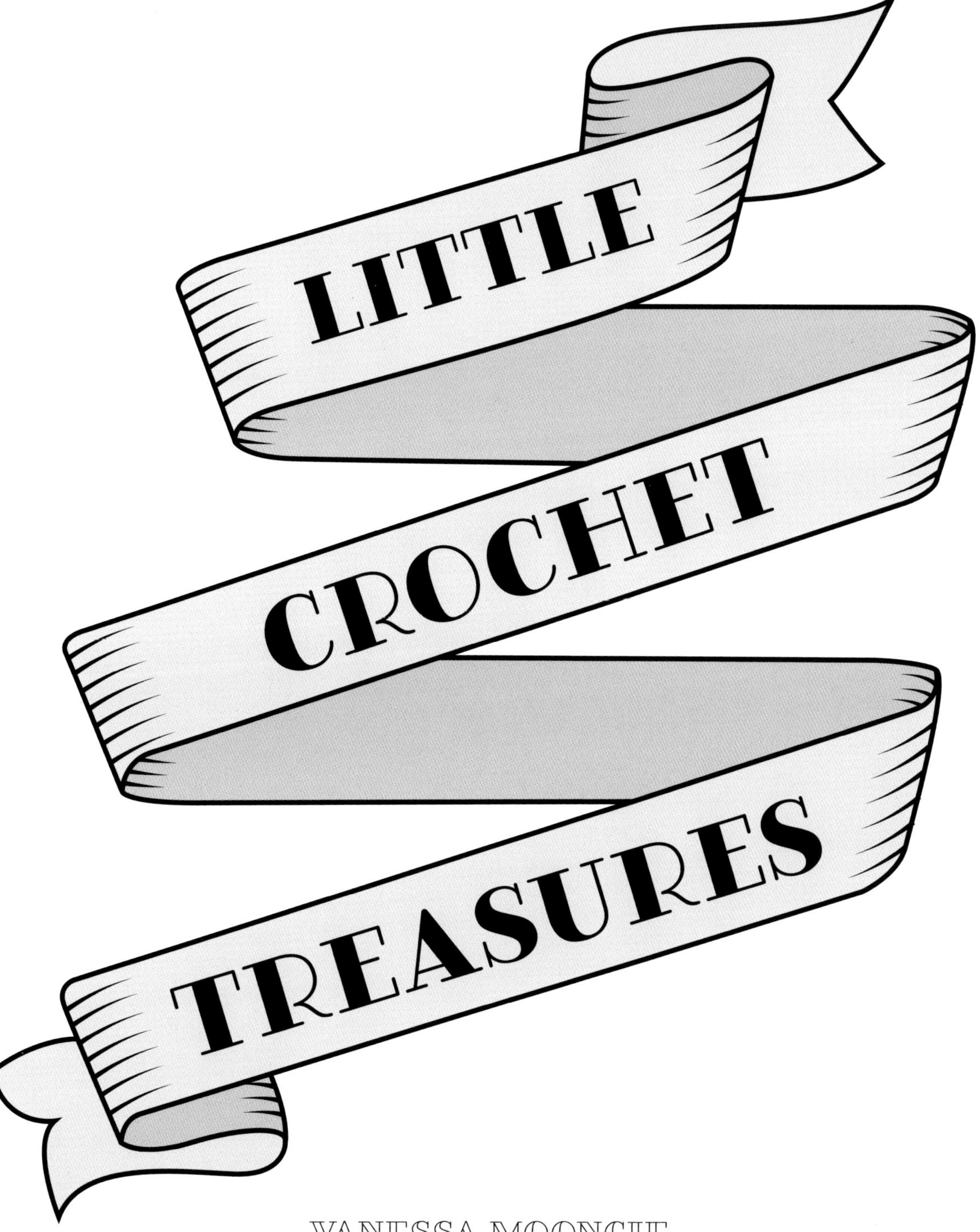

VANESSA MOONCIE

CONTENTS

INTRODUCTION

Little Crochet Treasures is a collection of 18 versatile projects to accessorize your hair and wardrobe. There are tips on adapting the pieces to produce variations of the original designs, such as making the charms of the bracelet into keyrings and creating a tie pin by modifying the cufflink pattern.

The book features a giant poppy hair corsage, target cufflinks, traditional tattoo-inspired anchors and hearts, and a delicate posy brooch, influenced by my small collection of vintage porcelain flower jewellery.

A variety of stitches feature in the projects using a range of fibres and textures, from fine threads to thicker yarns, together with various sized hooks. Finishing touches include the addition of beads, sequins and simple embroidery. All of the projects have charts to accompany the written instructions to make it easy to follow the patterns. At the front of the book there is information on the materials and tools needed for the projects, and illustrated step-by-step instructions on the crochet stitches used and working in multiple colours.

This book was first published as *Crocheted Accessories* in 2012 and has been revamped with beautiful photographs and a fresh new look. There are also some changes to a few projects, including instructions to make an acorn buttonhole and an updated version of the fantail dove pattern. The accessories are designed to use up leftover yarn from previous projects and most take very small amounts. These Little Crochet Treasures will make unique and cherished gifts for loved ones, or for yourself.

Vanessa

 PAGE 60

 PAGE 68

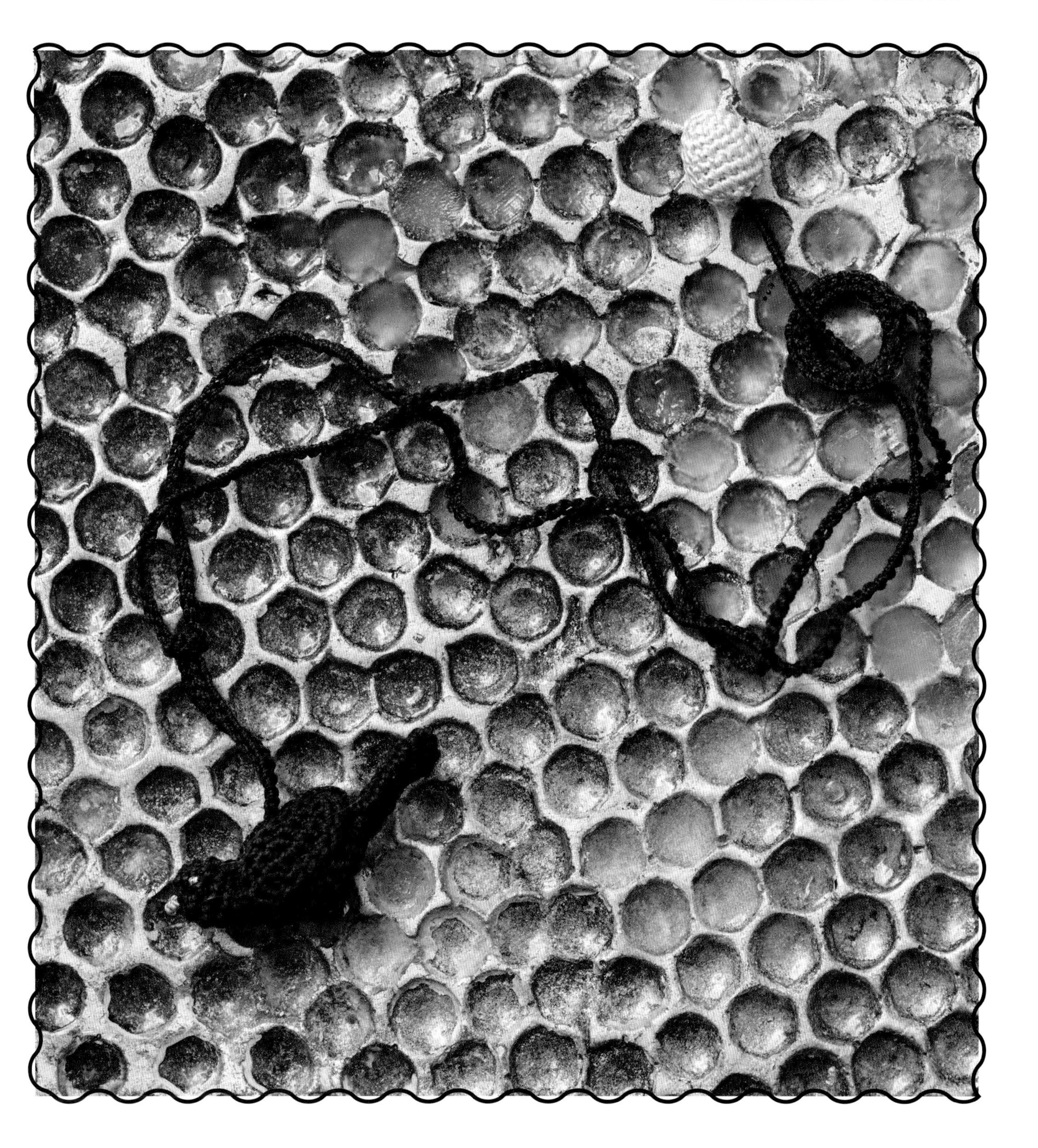

 PAGE 80

 PAGE 86

WILD STRAWBERRY PAGE 92

 PAGE 98

 PAGE 106

BUMBLEBEE PAGE 134

 PAGE 140

MOD TARGETS PAGE 146

GETTING STARTED

CM 1 2 3 4 5 6 7 8 9 10

EQUIPMENT & MATERIALS

The texture or colour of a yarn or thread can spark the start of an idea that, together with a small collection of simple and inexpensive tools, can be crocheted into a beautiful and unique accessory.

EQUIPMENT

Crocheting beautiful accessories requires only a few basic items of equipment. Hooks, of course, are the main requirement.

Crochet hooks

Originally, there were two ranges of hooks available in the UK – one for cotton and one for wool. A standard range for all thicknesses was then introduced in 1969. The old UK sizes are listed in the middle column of the chart overleaf. These sizes are not commonly used now, but might be handy to refer to if you are working from a vintage pattern or using vintage hooks. Metric hook sizes are listed on the left-hand side of the chart, while the US system of crochet hook sizing is given in the right-hand column. In this book we use metric hook sizes, but the UK and US equivalents are also given.

Crochet hooks traditionally come in aluminium and steel. They are also now commonly available in bamboo and in carved wood.

Hooks are available in a wide range of sizes: from 0.6mm (UK6:US14) to 1.75mm (UK2:US6) for use with fine threads; from 2mm (UK14:US-) to 11.5mm (UK-:USP/16) for thicker yarns; and enormous, outsized hooks for use with multiple strands of yarn.

Scissors

Small, sharp thread or embroidery scissors are best for trimming yarn ends, especially on delicate pieces.

Needles

Blunt-ended yarn needles are used to finish off the work in 4ply yarns. The rounded end prevents snagging. For projects using threads, a fine sewing needle with a sharp point is recommended. A thimble will come in handy, as it can be hard to get the needle through smaller pieces with compacted stuffing and closely woven stitches. Jewellery pliers are also a useful tool for this.

Pliers

There are three useful types of pliers:

- **Round-nose pliers**, for bending and looping the wire that decorates a finished piece of work.
- **Side cutters**, for cutting and trimming wires.
- **Flat-nose pliers**, for gripping wire and opening and closing wire rings. These are handy for use with both the round-nose and side-cutting pliers to hold fiddly wires while shaping and trimming them. They are also useful for pulling a needle through fine crocheted work.

MATERIALS

Beautiful yarns and threads, along with materials for embellishments such as beads, will feed your imagination and inspiration for making inventive crochet pieces.

Yarns and threads

There is an abundance of beautiful yarns and threads available, and experimenting with different textures and materials can be very inspiring. An idea may evolve just by seeing how the fibre takes on a form while crocheting a simple swatch. Vintage threads that are faded or discoloured will give a unique finish. The same design crocheted once in mohair and again in a metallic yarn will have a completely different appearance and tactile quality, as would working both fibres together.

Materials do not have to be restricted to traditional wools, cottons and linens. String, strips of fabric, recycled carrier bags, ribbons and wire are just a few of the found objects that have the potential to create a work of art. Embroidery threads are lovely to work with, as they are available in many jewel-like colours and the strands can be separated to make finer pieces.

The tensions (or gauges) and the sizes for the projects in this book are given just as a guide. Trying projects using different hooks and materials will alter the proportions as well as the measurements. Working with fine thread and a larger hook will produce an open, lacy, loopy stitch, whereas a tighter, stiffer fabric will be constructed with a thicker yarn and finer hook.

Beads and findings

A piece of crochet can be enhanced by adding a little sparkle with a single faceted glass bead. Semi-precious gems, pearls, shells, metal, wood or acrylic beads will change the finished look of the crocheted accessory. Threading a bead onto a head pin to hang from a crocheted pendant provides an alternative to stitching the decoration and creates a more professional finish overall. From recycling a broken vintage necklace or attaching a single charm, the project can be transformed to create a personal piece or treasured gift.

Brooch bars come in varying sizes and in gold or silver colour, for use according to the dimensions of the work and the desired finish. Bars can be widely found in nickel-plated, silver-plated or gold-plated metal and in sterling silver, with drilled holes for stitching through, or without holes – these can be attached by sewing around the bar.

Toy stuffing

Polyester fibre toy stuffing is ideal for filling the crocheted pieces to give a solid, three-dimensional form.

PVA glue

PVA (polyvinyl acetate) glue is perfect for stiffening the crocheted work and keeping it in shape. It is water-soluble and can be diluted if required. PVA is washable, though if a finished crocheted accessory goes through the wash, it will need reshaping and a fresh coating of the glue applied to revitalize it.

STEEL CROCHET HOOK CONVERSION

Metric (mm)	UK	US [C]
0.6	6	14
-	5½	13
0.75	5	12
-	4½	11
1	4	10
-	3½	9
1.25	3	8
1.50	2½	7
1.75	2	6
-	1½	5

ALUMINIUM CROCHET HOOK CONVERSION

Metric (mm)	UK	US [C]
2	14	-
2.25	13	B/1
2.5	12	-
2.75	-	C/2
3	11	-
3.25	10	D/3
3.5	9	E/4
3.75	-	F/5
4.	8	G/6
4.5	7	7
5	6	H/8
5.5	5	I/9
6	4	J/10
6.5	3	K/10½
7	2	-
8	0	L/11
9	00	M/13
10	000	N/15
11.5	-	P/16

TECHNIQUES

Crochet patterns are based on a few basic stitches. With just a hook and some yarn, starting with a simple slip knot, these stitches will provide endless possibilities for new designs and inspiration.

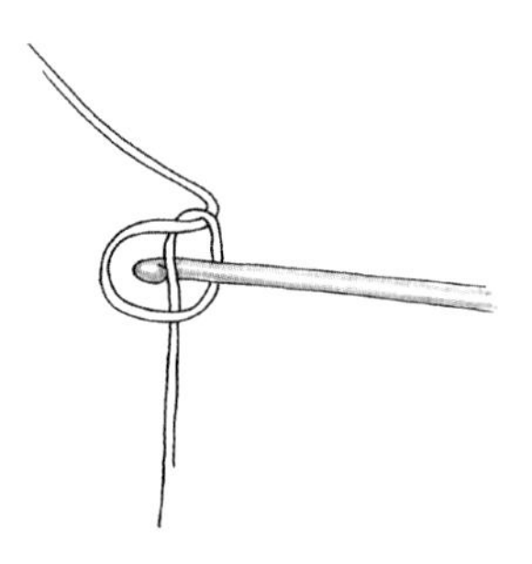

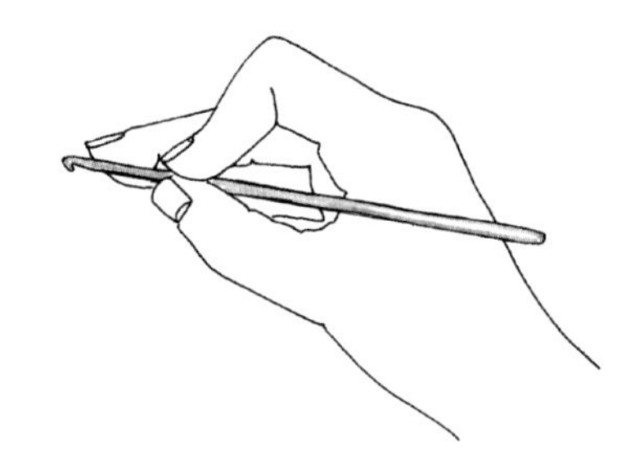

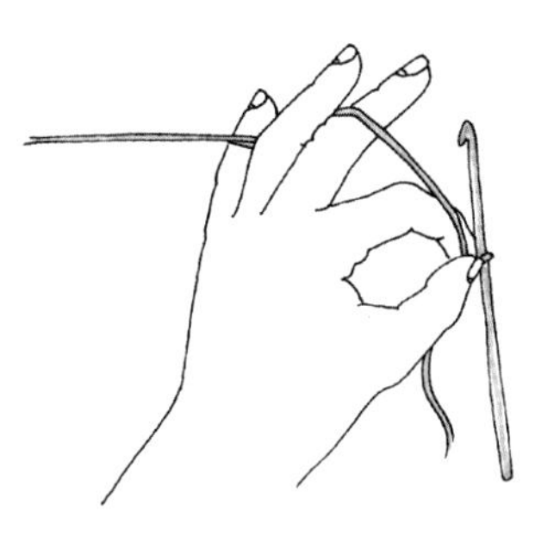

SLIP KNOT

Take the end of the yarn and form it into a loop. Holding it in place between thumb and forefinger, insert the hook through the loop, catch the long end that is attached to the ball, and draw it back through. Keeping the yarn looped on the hook, pull through until the loop closes around the hook, ensuring it is not tight. Pulling on the short end of yarn will loosen the knot, while pulling on the long end will tighten it.

HOLDING THE WORK

HOOK

Hold the hook as you would a pencil, bringing your middle finger forward to rest near the tip of the hook. This will help control the movement of the hook, while the fingers of your other hand will regulate the tension of the yarn. The hook should face you, pointing slightly downwards. The motion of the hook and yarn should be free and even, not tight. This will come with practice.

YARN

To hold your work and control the tension, pass the yarn over the first two fingers of your left hand (right if you are left-handed), under the third finger and around the little finger, and let the yarn fall loosely to the ball. As you work, take the stitch you made between the thumb and forefinger of the same hand.

The hook is usually inserted through the top two loops of a stitch as you work, unless otherwise stated in a pattern. A different effect is produced when only the back or front loop of the stitch is picked up.

MAGIC LOOP

Some of the projects start with an adjustable loop of yarn. To make the loop, wind the yarn around a finger, insert the hook, catch the yarn and draw back though the loop. After a couple of rounds have been crocheted, covering the loop of yarn, the short end of yarn is pulled tight to close the centre. The other method used is to make four chain stitches and then slip stitch to the first chain to form a ring. However, this technique does leave a small hole in the middle.

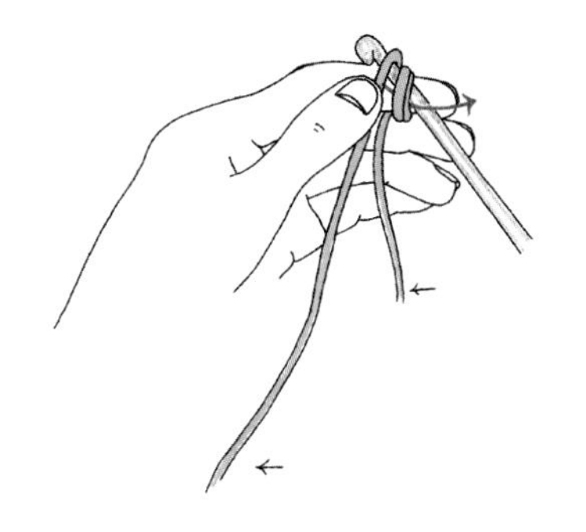

CHAIN (CH)

1. Pass the hook under and over the yarn that is held taut between the first and second fingers. This is called 'yarn round hook' (yrh). Draw the yarn through the loop on the hook. This makes one chain (ch).

2. Repeat step 1, keeping the thumb and forefinger of the left hand close to the hook, until you have as many chain stitches as required.

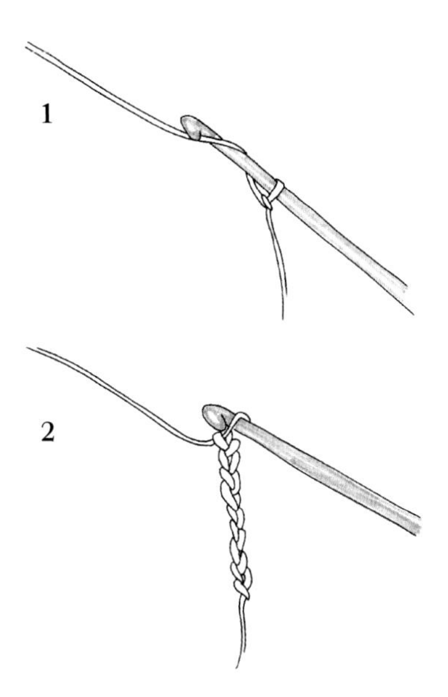

SLIP STITCH (SL ST)

Make a practice chain of 10. Insert hook into first stitch (st), yrh, draw through both loops on hook. This forms 1 slip stitch (sl st). Continue to end. This will give you 10 slip stitches (10 sts).

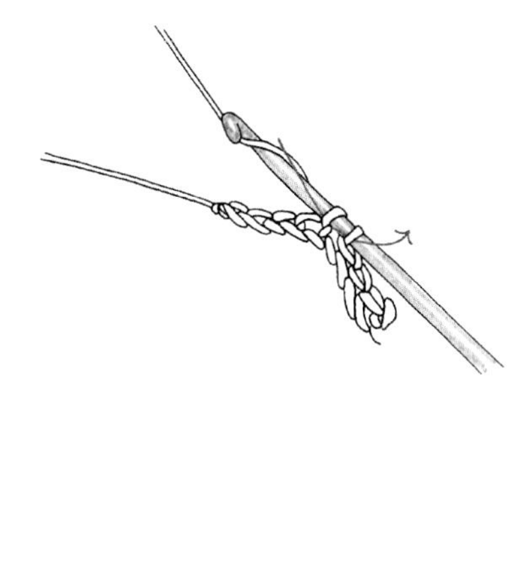

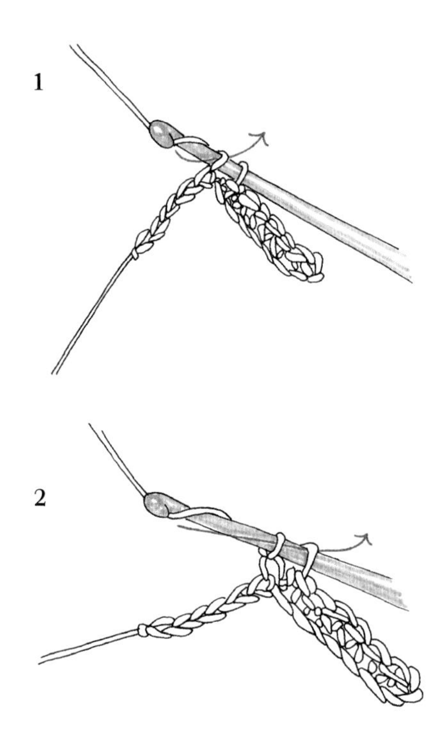

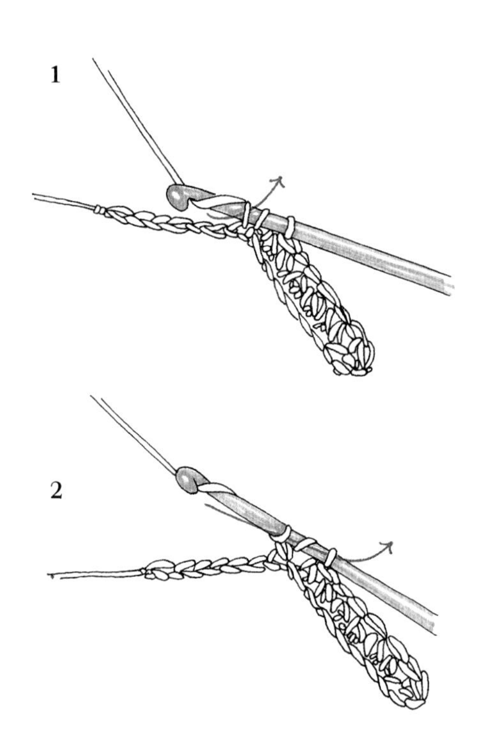

DOUBLE CROCHET (DC)

Make a practice chain of 17. Skip the first ch.
1. Insert hook from front into the next stitch, yrh and draw back through the stitch (two loops on hook).

2. Yrh and draw through two loops (one loop on hook). This makes one double crochet (dc).
Repeat steps 1 and 2 to the end of the row. On the foundation chain of 17 sts, you should have 16 double crochet sts (16 sts).

Next row

Turn the work so the reverse side faces you. Make 1 ch. This is the turning chain; it helps keep a neat edge and does not count as a stitch. Repeat steps 1 and 2 to the end of the row. Continue until the desired number of rows is complete. Fasten off.

FASTENING OFF

When you have finished, fasten off by cutting the yarn around 4¾in (12cm) from the work. Draw the loose end through the remaining loop, pulling it tightly.

HALF TREBLE (HTR)

Make a practice chain of 17. Skip the first 2 ch (these count as the first half treble stitch).
1. Yrh, insert hook into the next stitch, yrh and draw back through stitch (three loops on hook).

2. Yrh, draw through all three loops (one loop on hook). This forms 1 half treble (htr).

Repeat steps 1 and 2 to the end of the row.

On the foundation chain of 17 sts, you should have 16 half trebles (16 sts), including the 2 ch at the beginning of the row, which is counted as the first stitch.

Next row

Turn the work so the reverse side faces you. Make 2 ch to count as the first half treble. Skip the first stitch of the previous row. Repeat steps 1 and 2 for the next 14 htr of the last row, work 1 htr in the second of the 2 ch at the end of the row. Continue until the desired number of rows is complete. Fasten off.

TREBLE (TR)

Make a practice chain of 18. Skip the first 3 ch (these count as the first tr).

1. Yrh, insert hook into the next stitch, yrh and draw back through the stitch (three loops on hook).

2. Yrh, draw through two loops (two loops on hook).

3. Yrh, draw through two loops (one loop on hook). This forms 1 treble (tr).

Repeat steps 1–3 to the end of the row.

On the foundation chain of 18 sts, you should have 16 trebles (16 sts), including the 3 ch at the beginning of the row, which is counted as the first stitch.

Next row

Turn the work so the reverse side faces you. Make 3 ch to count as the first treble. Skip the first stitch of the previous row. Repeat steps 1–3 to the end of the row, working 1 tr into the third of the 3 ch at the beginning of the last row. Continue until the desired number of rows is complete. Fasten off.

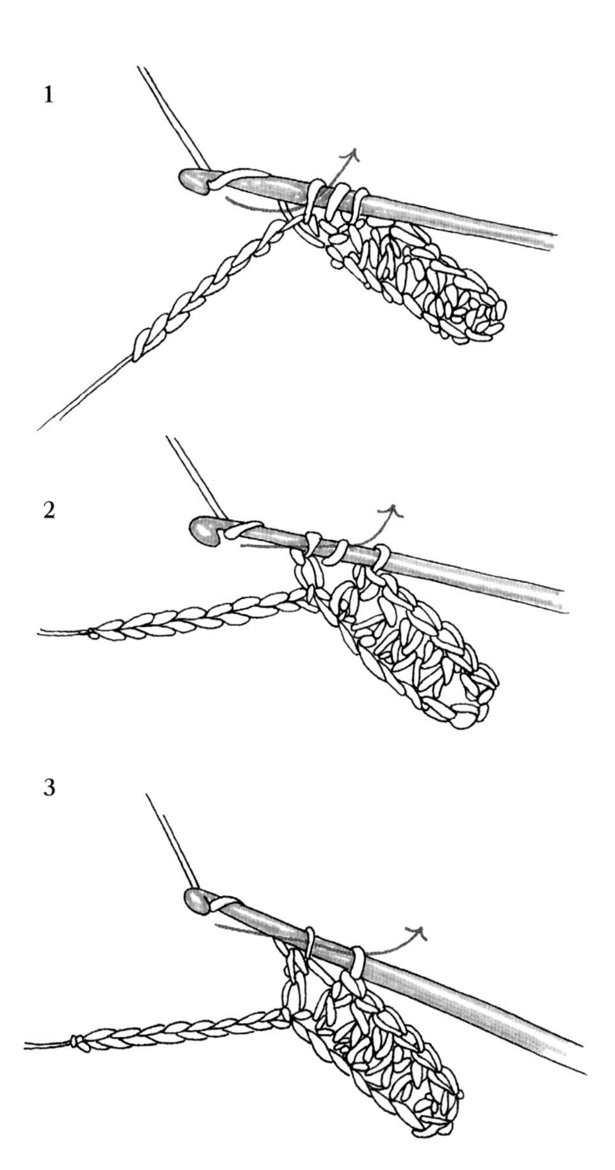

DOUBLE TREBLE (DTR)

Make a practice chain of 19. Skip the first 4 ch (these count as the first double treble stitch).

1. (Yrh) twice, insert hook into the next st, yrh and draw back through stitch (4 loops on hook).

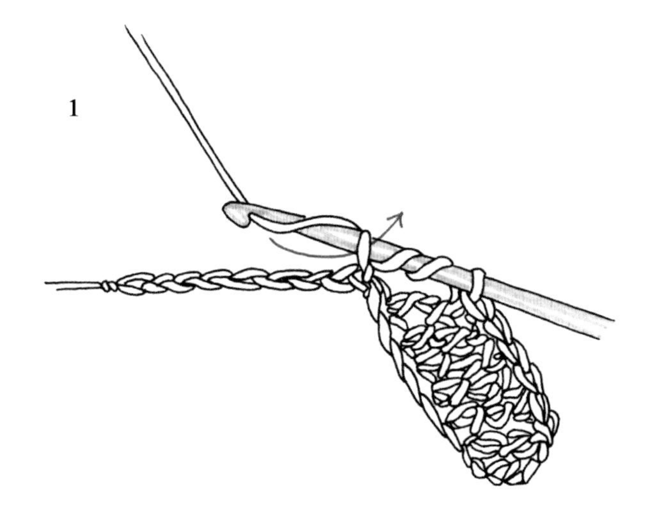

2. (Yrh, draw through 2 loops) 3 times (1 loop on hook). This forms 1 double treble (dtr).

Repeat steps 1 and 2 to the end of the row.

On the foundation chain of 19 sts you should have 16 double trebles (16 sts), including the 4 ch at the beginning of the row, counted as the first stitch.

Next row

Turn the work so the reverse side faces you. Make 4 ch to count as the first double treble. Skip the first stitch of the previous row. Repeat steps 1 and 2 to the end of the row, working 1 dtr into the fourth of the 4 ch. Continue until you have completed the desired number of rows. Fasten off.

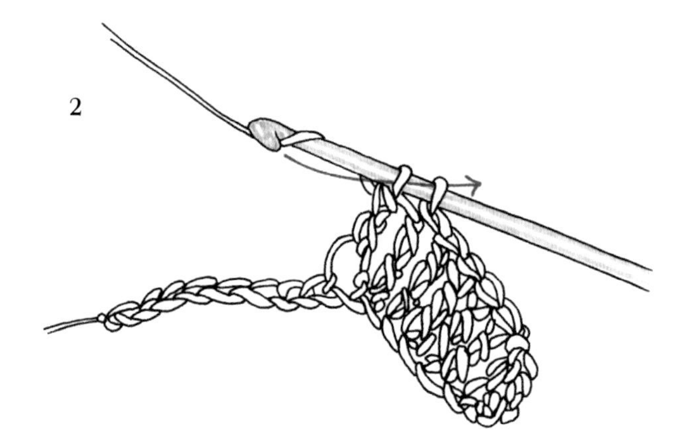

TRIPLE TREBLE (TRTR)

Make a practice chain of 20. Skip the first 5 ch (these count as the first triple treble stitch).
1. (Yrh) three times, insert hook into the next st, yrh and draw back through stitch (5 loops on hook).

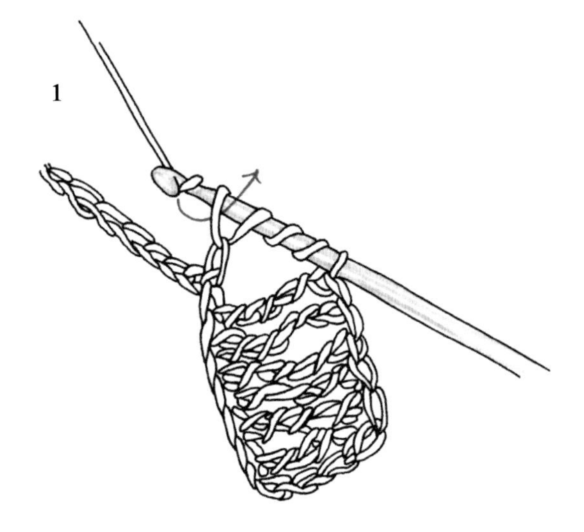

2. (Yrh, draw through 2 loops) 4 times (1 loop on hook). This forms 1 triple treble (trtr).

Repeat steps 1 and 2 to the end of the row.

On the foundation chain of 20 sts you should have 16 triple trebles (16 sts), including the 5 ch at the beginning of the row, counted as the first stitch.

Next row

Turn the work so the reverse side faces you. Make 5 ch to count as the first triple treble. Skip the first stitch of the previous row. Repeat steps 1 and 2 to the end of the row, working 1 trtr into the fifth of the 5 ch. Continue until you have completed the desired number of rows. Fasten off.

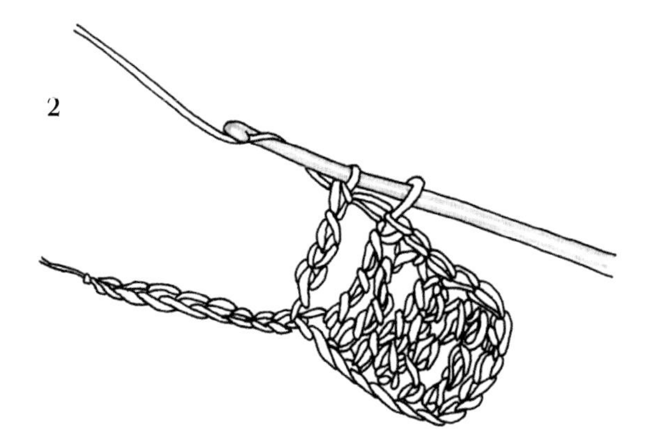

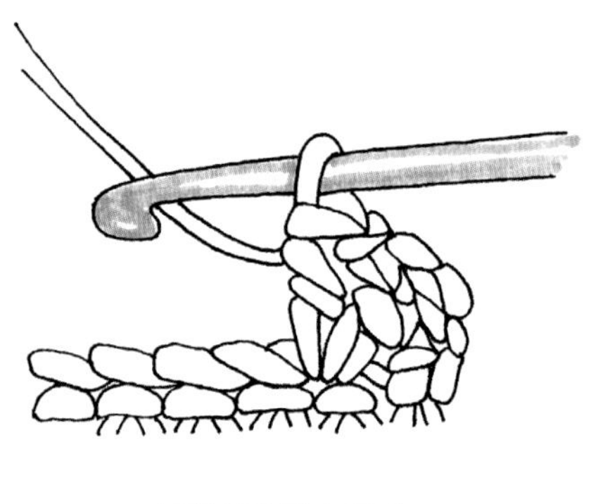

INCREASE

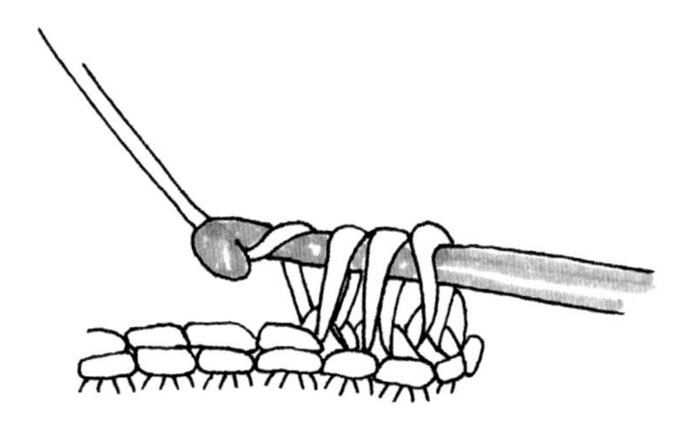

DECREASE

INCREASING

To increase one double crochet (dc2inc), one half treble (htr2inc), one treble stitch (tr2inc), one double treble (dtr) or one triple treble (trtr), work two stitches into one stitch of the previous row. To increase two double treble stitches (dtr3inc), work three stitches into one stitch of the previous row.

DECREASING

Decrease one double crochet (dc2tog)

1. Insert the hook into the next st, yrh and draw back through the stitch (two loops on hook).
2. Insert the hook into the following st, yrh and draw back through the st (three loops on hook).
3. Yrh and draw through all three loops.

Decrease one half treble (htr2tog)

1. Yrh, insert the hook into the next st, yrh and draw back through the stitch (three loops on hook).
2. Yrh, insert the hook into the following st, yrh and draw back through the st (five loops on hook).
3. Yrh and draw through all five loops.

Decrease two treble stitches (tr3tog)

1–2. Follow steps 1–2 of treble stitch.
3. Yrh, insert hook into the following stitch, yrh and draw back through the stitch (four loops on hook).
4. Yrh, draw through two loops (three loops on hook).
5–6. Repeat steps 3–4 (four loops on hook)
7. Yrh, draw through all four loops.

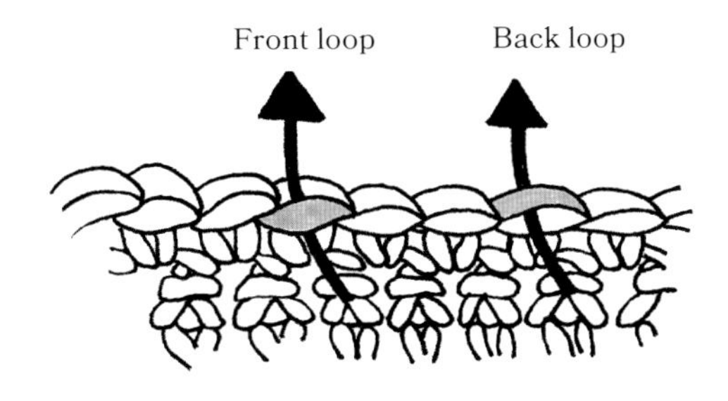

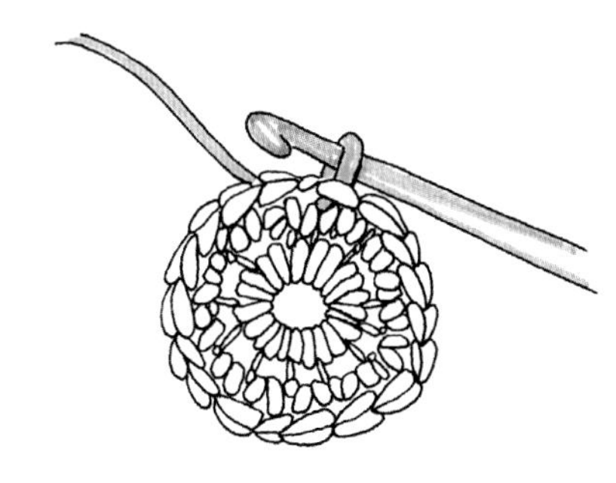

JOINING A NEW COLOUR AT THE BEGINNING OF A ROUND

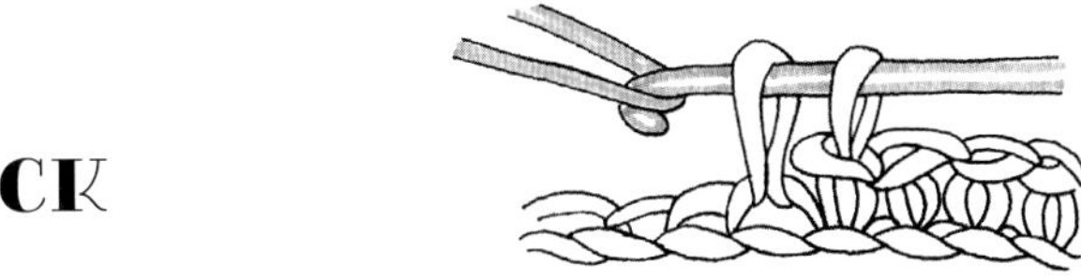

JOINING A NEW COLOUR IN THE MIDDLE OF A ROW

WORKING INTO THE BACK OR FRONT LOOP ONLY

The front loop of a stitch is the one closer to you; the back loop is the stitch further away. Generally, the hook is inserted into both loops of a stitch, but when only one loop is crocheted into, the horizontal bar of the remaining loop is left on the surface of the fabric. This method is used to produce the corrugated effect of the simple cupcake case on page 127.

WORKING WITH MULTIPLE COLOURS

Joining a new colour

When joining in a new colour at the beginning of a round or middle of a row, work the last step of the stitch in the new colour. Catch the yarn in the new colour and draw through the loops on the hook to complete the stitch.

Carrying unused yarn across the work

When the colour that is not in use is to be carried across the wrong side of the work, it can be hidden along the line of stitches being made by working over the unused strand every few stitches with the new colour. When both sides of the work will be visible, the unused strand is worked over on every stitch, keeping the crocheted fabric neat on both sides. Lay the strand not being used on top of the previous row of stitches and crochet over it in the new colour, covering the unused colour.

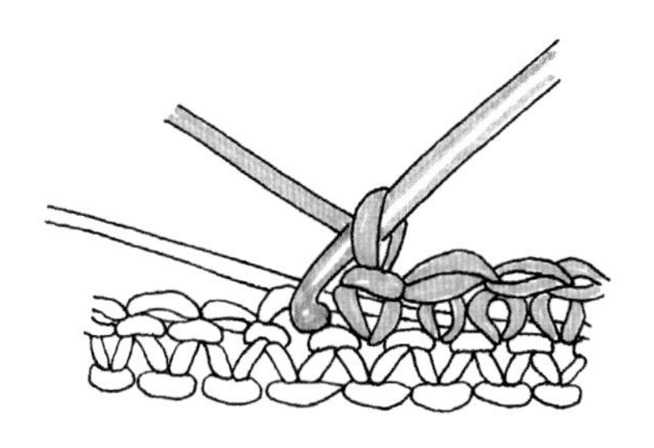

CARRYING UNUSED YARN ACROSS THE WORK

BROOCHES

SWEETHEART TATTOO

A blend of stitches, colour and texture form the symbols of the rose and the heart in a celebration of love. Here the two combine to create a traditional-style tattoo brooch.

MATERIALS

- Small amount of 4ply yarn in red (A), oddments of 4ply yarn in cream (B), pale yellow (C), bright blue (D), dark blue (E), pale pink (F), bright pink (G) and metallic black (H)
- 2.5mm (UK12:US-) crochet hook
- Small amount of toy stuffing
- Blunt-ended yarn needle
- 1¼in (3cm) brooch bar

SIZE

Widest part measures approximately 2¾in (7cm) excluding flowers
Longest part measures approximately 2⅛in (5.5cm)

TENSION

26 sts and 26 rows to 4in (10cm) over double crochet using 2.5mm hook and A.
Use larger or smaller hook if necessary to obtain correct tension.

METHOD

The heart is crocheted in continuous rounds. The ribbon is worked in rows, decreasing then increasing the stitches at each end to form the shaping. The roses are formed from a length of crocheted scalloped petals, which, when wound into a spiral, creates the finished bloom.

NOTE

1 ch at beg of the row/ round does not count as a st throughout.

HEART

With 2.5mm hook and A, make a magic loop.

Round 1: 1 ch, 6 dc (6 sts).

Round 2: 1 dc in each st.

Pull tightly on short end of yarn to close loop.

Round 3 (inc): (Dc2inc) 6 times (12 sts).

Round 4: 1 dc in each st.

Round 5 (inc): (Dc2inc) 12 times (24 sts).

Rounds 6–7: 1 dc in each st.

Round 8 (inc): (Dc2inc, 1 dc) 12 times (36 sts).

Rounds 9–10: 1 dc in each st.

KEY

- chain (ch)
- double crochet (dc)
- dc2inc
- dc2tog
- treble (tr)

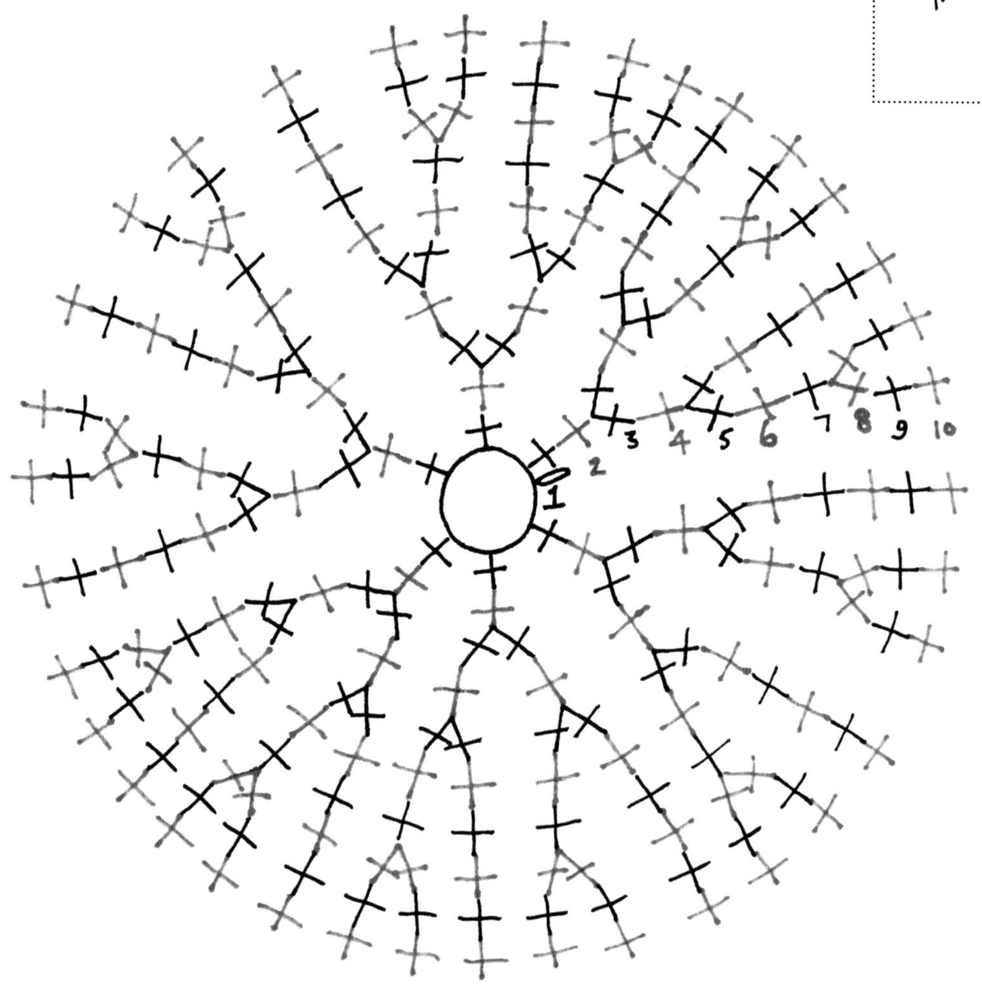

HEART ROUNDS 1–10

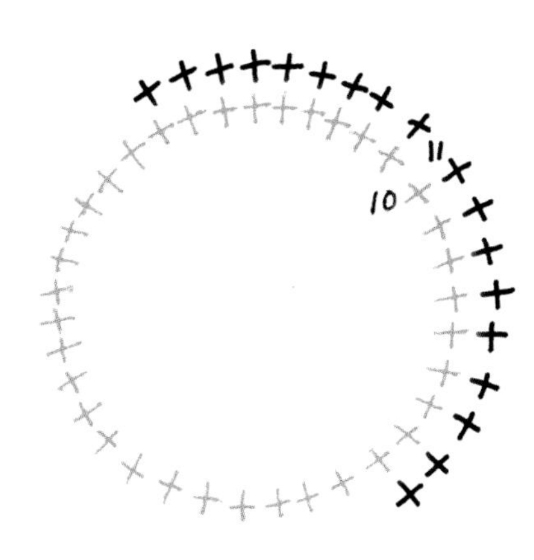

SHAPE TOP ROUND 11

SHAPE TOP ROUNDS 12–14

Shape top

****Round 11:** 1 dc in each of next 9 dc, skip next 18 sts, 1 dc in next 9 dc.
Continue on these 18 sts.
Rounds 12–14: 1 dc in each st.
Fasten off, leaving a long tail of yarn. With RS facing, join A with a sl st to the first of the unworked 18 sts. Starting in the same dc as the sl st, work 4 rounds of 1 dc in each st to match the first side. Fasten off, leaving a long tail of yarn. Stuff the heart firmly, thread the tail of yarn through the stitches of the last round, pull tightly on the yarn to close the opening and fasten off. Repeat to finish the other side of the top shaping. Weave in all the ends.**

RIBBON

With 2.5mm hook and H, make 38 ch.
Row 1 (dec): 1 dc into 3rd ch from hook, 1 dc in each of next 33 ch, dc2tog, turn (35 sts).
Row 2 (dec): Skip the first dc, 1 dc in next 32 dc, dc2tog, turn (33 sts).
Row 3 (inc): 3 ch, 1 dc in 2nd and 3rd ch from hook, 1 dc in next 33 dc, turn (35 sts).
Row 4 (inc): 3 ch, 1 dc into 2nd and 3rd ch from hook, 1 dc in next 34 dc, sl st to next st (37 sts).
Fasten off.

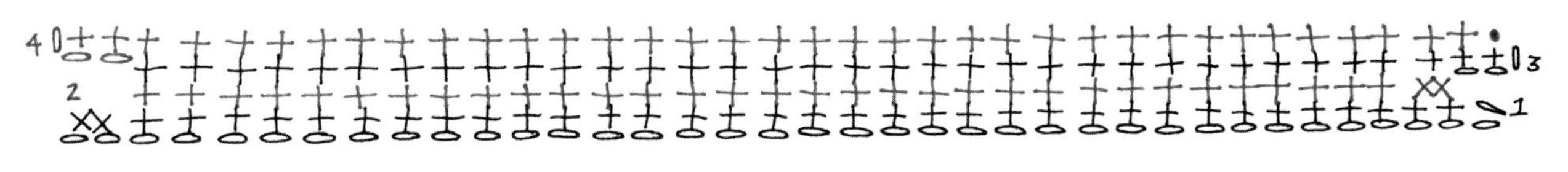

RIBBON

ROSE (MAKE 3)

With 2.5mm hook and B, make 8 ch.
Row 1: 1 dc into 2nd ch from hook, (4 ch, 1 dc in next ch) 6 times, turn (6 4-ch sps, 6 sts).
Row 2: *(1 dc, 8 tr, 1 dc) in next 4-ch sp*; rep from * to * 3 more times. Join C in last dc and rep from * to * twice with C. Fasten off, leaving a long tail of yarn. Weave in the ends. With WS of work on the inside, wind the petals into a tight spiral and sew a few stitches to secure it in place, using the tail of yarn left after fastening off.
Make a rose using D with E and another using F with G, in place of B and C.

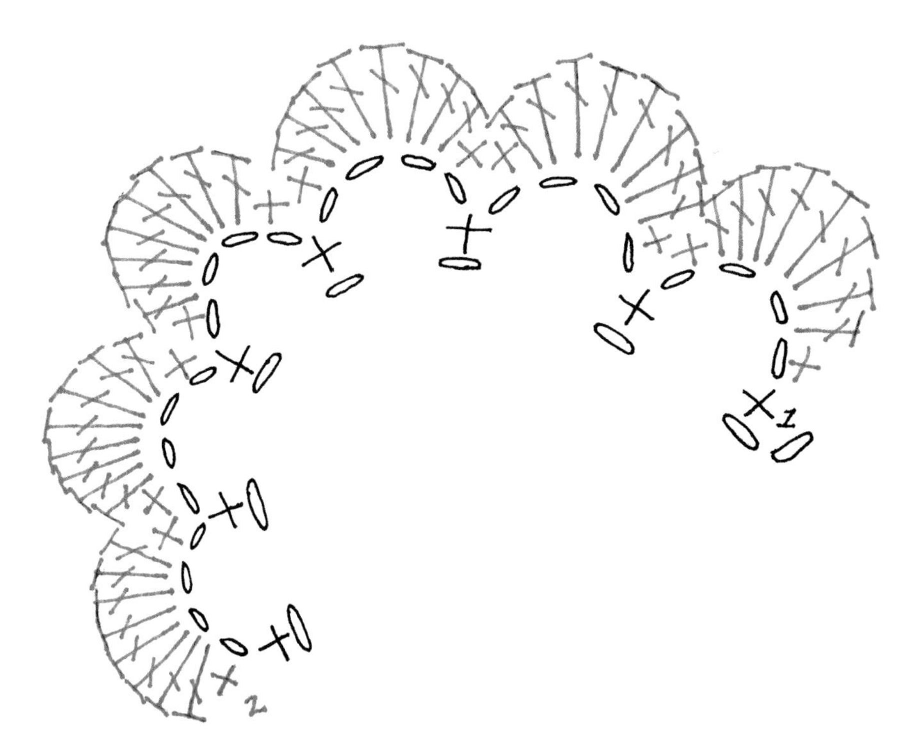

ROSE

MAKING UP

The ribbon can be embroidered with a name or word, if so desired, such as 'sweet', 'true' or 'love', using embroidery threads or seed beads before attaching it to the finished heart. Position the ribbon over the heart at a slight angle, from the left going down to the right, wrapping it around the sides to the back and folding both ends towards the front again to give the draped effect. Stitch in place (see illustration below). Sew the roses to the left side and attach a brooch bar to the back, placing it just below the top shaping. Paint a thin layer of PVA glue on the backs of the shaped ends of the ribbon to keep them in shape. Leave to dry completely before wearing.

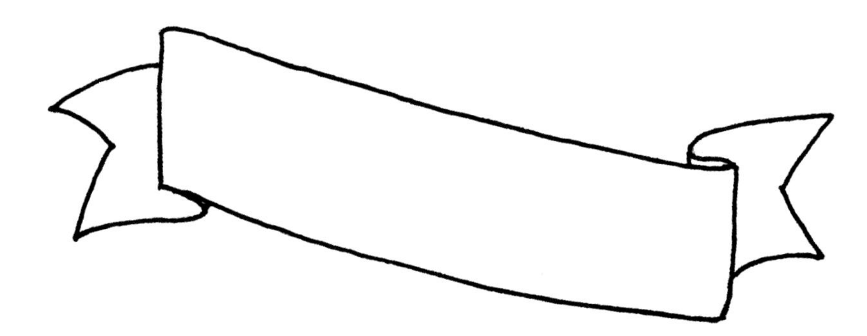

VARIATION:
SIMPLE BROOCH

Make a simple version of the sweetheart tattoo brooch by following rows 1 to 9 of the pattern as given for the heart. Omit row 10 and continue from ** to **.

Make the ribbon, as before, and attach it across the finished, smaller heart in the same way. Attach a brooch bar to the back of the heart, just below the top shaping.

ANCHOR TATTOO

Ahoy there, sailor! This brooch brings together the stability and protection, symbolized by the anchor, with all the fun of the seaside.

MATERIALS

- Small amount of 4ply yarn in dark blue (A), oddments of 4ply in pale blue (B) (use DOUBLED) and metallic black (C)
- 2mm (UK14:US-) and 2.5mm (UK12:US-) crochet hooks
- Small amount of toy stuffing
- Blunt-ended yarn needle
- 1¼in (3cm) brooch bar

SIZE

Widest part measures approximately 3in (7.5cm)
Longest part measures approximately 3⅜in (8.5cm)

TENSION

26 sts and 26 rows to 4in (10cm) over double crochet using 2.5mm hook and A.
Use larger or smaller hook if necessary to obtain correct tension.

NOTE

1 ch at beg of the row/round does not count as a st throughout.

METHOD

Each piece of the anchor is made separately. The main parts are stuffed before stitching the pieces together. A simple length of crocheted chain is draped around the anchor, and a ribbon, worked in rows with the shaping formed by decreasing and increasing the stitches, is added to the front. A brooch bar attached to the back finishes the anchor.

ANCHOR SHANK

Starting at the base, with 2mm hook and A, make 4 ch and join with a sl st to first ch to form a ring.

Round 1: 1 ch, 5 dc into ring (5 sts).
Round 2: (Dc2inc) 5 times (10 sts).
Rounds 3–6: 1 dc in each st.
Round 7 (dec): (Dc2tog, 3 dc) twice (8 sts).
Rounds 8–16: 1 dc in each st.
Fasten off, leaving a long tail of yarn.

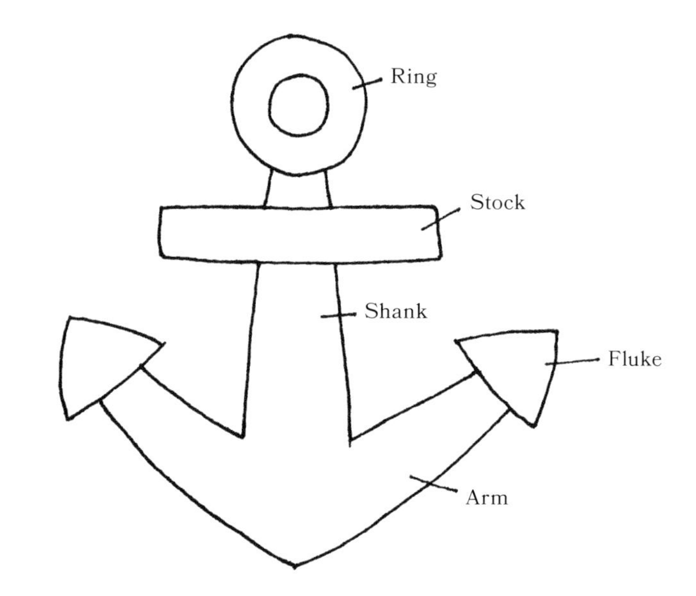

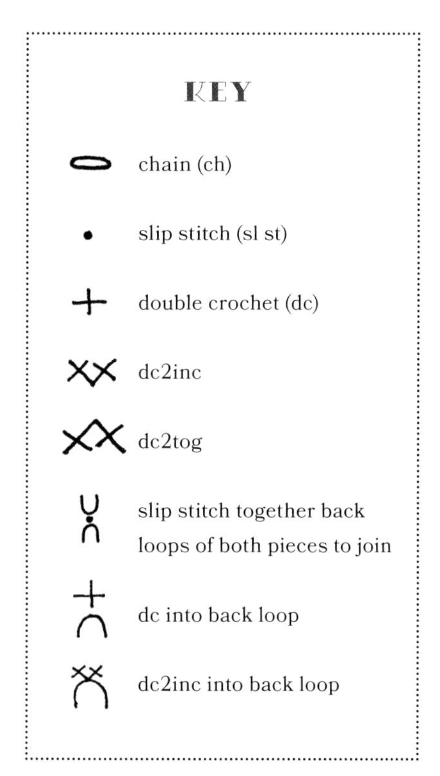

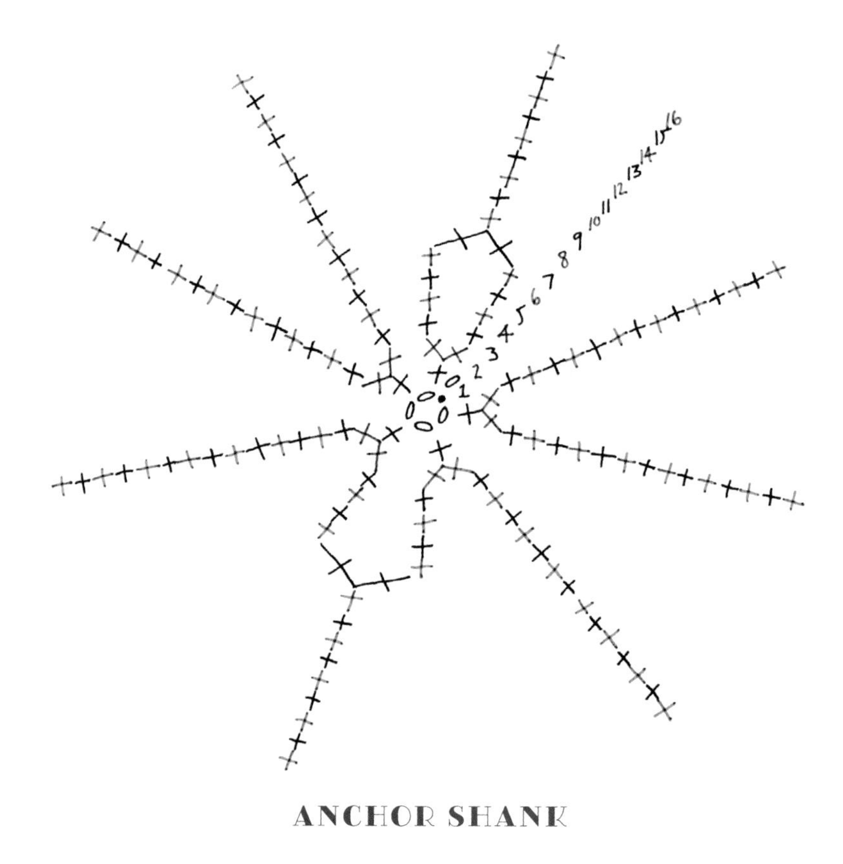

ANCHOR SHANK

STOCK

With 2mm hook and A, make a magic loop.

Round 1: 1 ch, 8 dc into loop (8 sts).

Rounds 2–5: 1 dc in each st.

Pull tightly on short end of yarn to close loop.

Divide for openings

The following is worked in rows:

Row 6: 1 dc in next 3 dc, turn, finishing 5 sts before the end of the row.

Continue on these 3 sts.

Rows 7–9: 1 ch, 1 dc in each dc, turn.

Fasten off.

Complete other side

With RS facing, skip the first of the 5 remaining sts on round 6 and join A with a sl st to the next st.

Next: Starting in the same dc as the sl st, rep rows 6–9.

Do not fasten off.

Join the two sides

The following is continued in rounds:

Round 10: With RS facing, 1 ch, *1 dc in next 3 dc, 1 ch*, continuing onto the other side of work to join, rep from * to *, sl st to first dc (8 sts).

Round 11: (1 dc in next 3 dc, 1 dc in next ch) twice.

Rounds 12–14: 1 dc in each dc.

Fasten off.

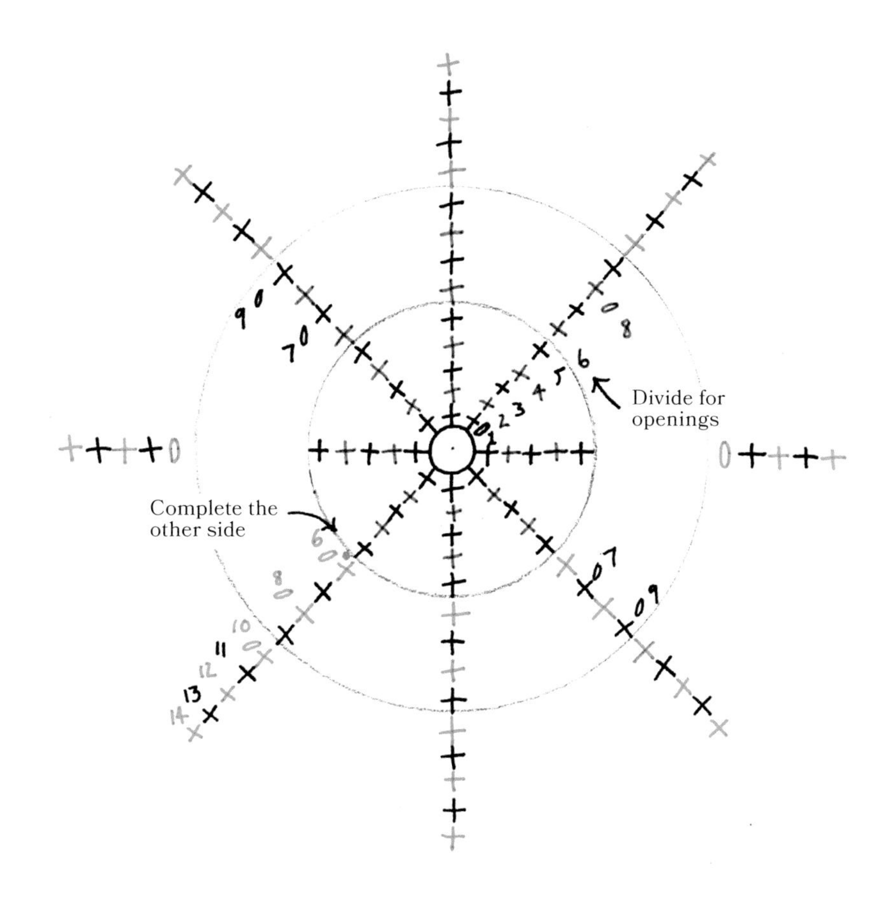

STOCK

RING (MAKE 2)

With 2.5mm hook and A, make 8 ch and join with sl st to first ch to form a ring.
Next: 1 ch, 24 dc into ring. Fasten off.
Make another ring to match the first, do not fasten off.

Join rings

Holding both pieces with WS tog, sl st into the back loops of the next 20 sts on both pieces at the same time to join. Fasten off, leaving a long tail of yarn.

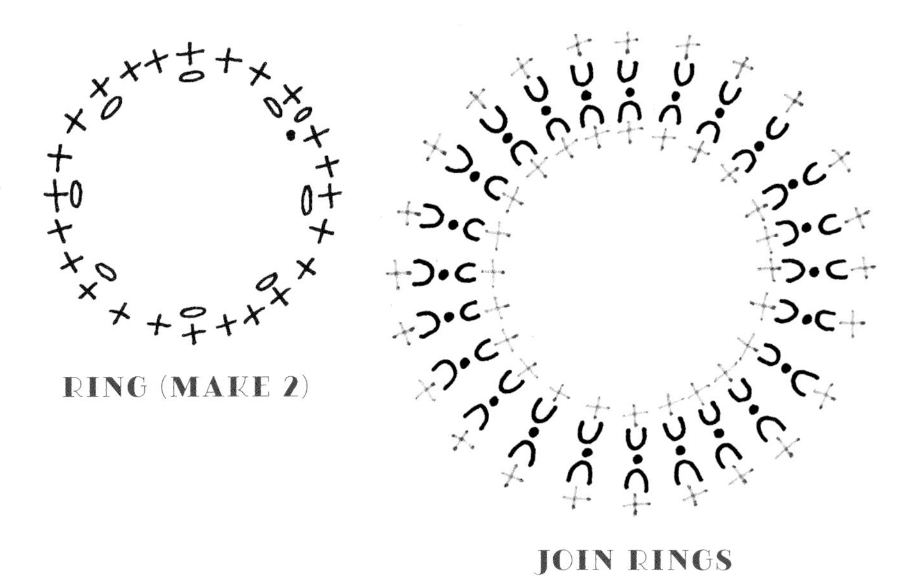

RING (MAKE 2)

JOIN RINGS

ARM

With 2mm hook and A, make 19 ch.
Row 1: 1 dc into 2nd ch from hook, 1 dc into next 17 ch, turn (18 sts).
Row 2 (inc): 1 ch, 1 dc in next 8 dc, (dc2inc) twice, 1 dc in next 8 dc, turn (20 sts).
Row 3 (inc): 1 ch, 1 dc in next 9 dc, (dc2inc) twice, 1 dc in next 9 dc, turn (22 sts).
Row 4 (dec): 1 ch, 1 dc in next 9 dc, (dc2tog) twice, 1 dc in next 9 dc, turn (20 sts).
Row 5 (dec): 1 ch, 1 dc in next 8 dc, (dc2tog) twice, 1 dc in next 8 dc, turn (18 sts).
Row 6: 1 dc in each dc. Fasten off.

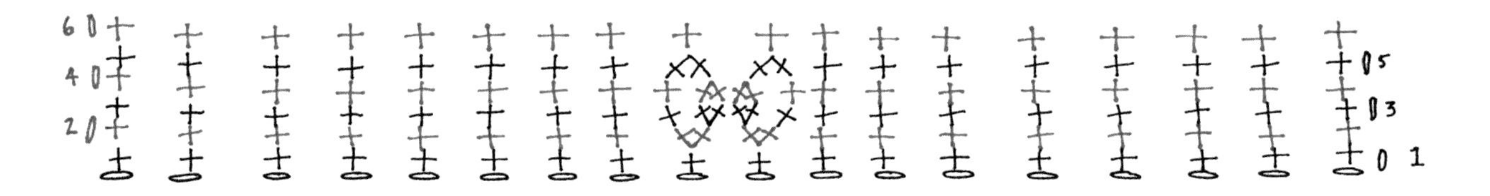

ARM

FLUKE (MAKE 2)

With 2mm hook and A, make a magic loop.

Round 1: 1 ch, 6 dc into loop (6 sts).

Round 2: 1 dc into back loop only of each dc.

Round 3: (Dc2inc, 1 dc) into back loops, 3 times (9 sts).

Round 4: (Dc2inc, 2 dc) into back loops, 3 times (12 sts).

Round 5: (Dc2inc, 2 dc) into back loops, 4 times (16 sts). Pull tightly on short end to close loop.

Fasten off, leaving a long tail of yarn.

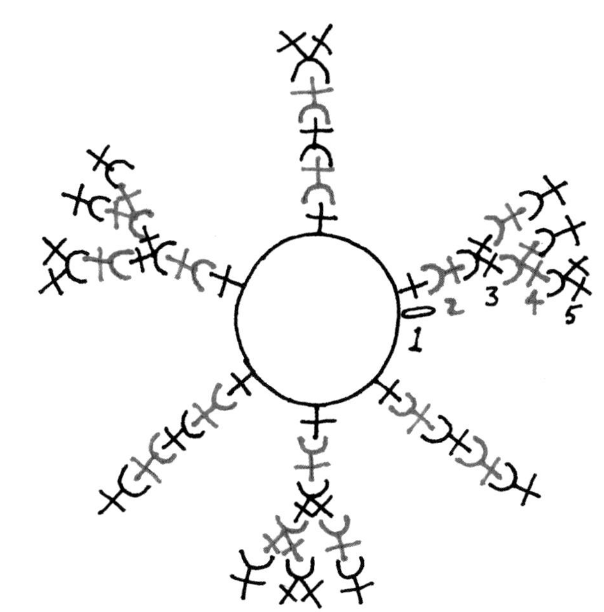

FLUKE (MAKE 2)

CHAIN

With 2.5mm hook and B DOUBLED, make 35 ch. Fasten off, leaving a long tail of yarn.

CHAIN

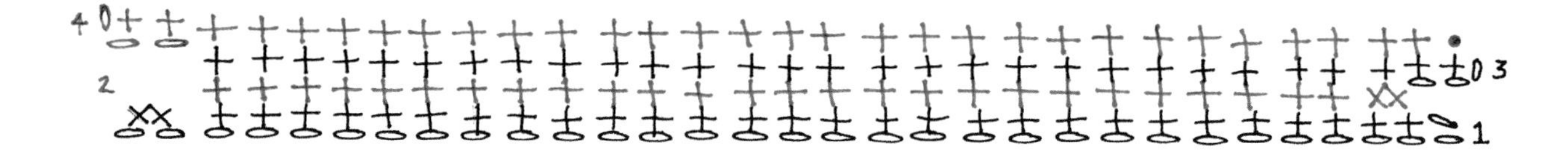

RIBBON

RIBBON

With 2mm hook and C, make 32 ch.

Row 1 (dec): 1 dc into 3rd ch from hook, 1 dc in next 27 ch, dc2tog, turn (29 sts).

Row 2 (dec): Skip the first dc, 1 dc in next 26 dc, dc2tog, turn (27 sts).

Row 3 (inc): 3 ch, 1 dc in 2nd and 3rd ch from hook, 1 dc in next 27 dc, turn (29 sts).

Row 4 (inc): 3 ch, 1 dc into 2nd and 3rd ch from hook, 1 dc in next 28 sts, sl st into next st (31 sts).

Fasten off.

A loved one's name, or a word such as 'true' or 'hope', can be added to the ribbon in embroidery or beading, or simply left blank, as desired.

MAKING UP

Stuff the shank using the end of the crochet hook to push the stuffing right into the base. Thread the tail of yarn through the last round, pull tightly to close the opening and fasten off. Stuff the first half of the stock, finishing at the opening in the middle. Slip the open centre of the stock over the narrow end of the shank and stitch in position ½in (1.25cm) from the top (see photograph opposite). Stuff the other end of the stock, gather the open end and fasten off.

Place the open end of the ring over the narrow top of the shank, and stitch in place. Fold the arm of the anchor and slip the wide end of the shank into the shaped centre of the arm. Stitch in place and then join the seams on each side. Stuff each side of the arm, teasing it back into shape as you go. Run a gathering stitch around each end, pull on the yarn to close and fasten off. Slip a fluke over one end of the arm so there is a gap on each side. Sew the overlapping edges together and slip stitch the fluke in place on the arm. Repeat to finish the other side.

Use the tail of yarn to attach the chain, draping it around the anchor and fixing in place with a few stitches. Fold the shaped edge on the right of the ribbon to the back then fold again to the front of the work so it sits above the upper edge. Repeat for the left side so it sits below the lower edge. Stitch the folded edges in position (see the illustration below) and sew the ribbon across the front of the anchor.

Weave in all the yarn ends. Sew a brooch bar across the back of the stock (see photograph, right).

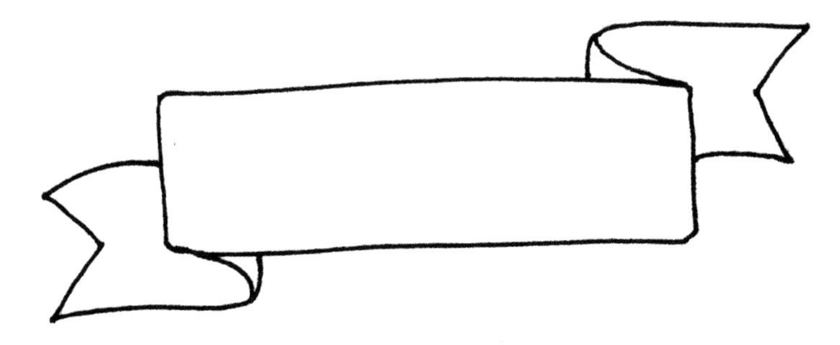

VARIATION

Make the anchor in the same way, omitting the ribbon, for an alternative look.

ICED DOUGHNUT

This jolly chocolate doughnut brooch is decorated with embroidered sprinkles scattered over pink crocheted icing, for a scrumptious looking treat to brighten up your wardrobe.

MATERIALS

- Small amount of DK yarn in brown (A)
- Small amount of 4ply yarn in pink (B)
- Oddments of embroidery thread in various colours to decorate
- 2.5mm (UK12:US-) crochet hook
- Small amount of toy stuffing
- Blunt-ended yarn needle
- 1¼in (3cm) brooch bar

SIZE

Approximately 2¼in (6.5cm) in diameter
Approximately ⅞in (2.25cm) deep

TENSION

26 sts and 26 rows to 4in (10cm) over double crochet using 2.5mm hook and A.
Use larger or smaller hook if necessary to obtain correct tension.

> **NOTE**
> **1 ch at beg of the row/round does not count as a st throughout.**

METHOD

The chocolate base is worked first, beginning at the centre of the ring. The pink icing is started by crocheting into the opposite side of the chain stitches of the doughnut base, and then continued in the same pattern. The open edges are joined by crocheting into both sets of stitches, stuffing the ring as you go. French knots (see page 59) decorate the iced top. Alternatively, seed beads can be stitched to the pink icing.

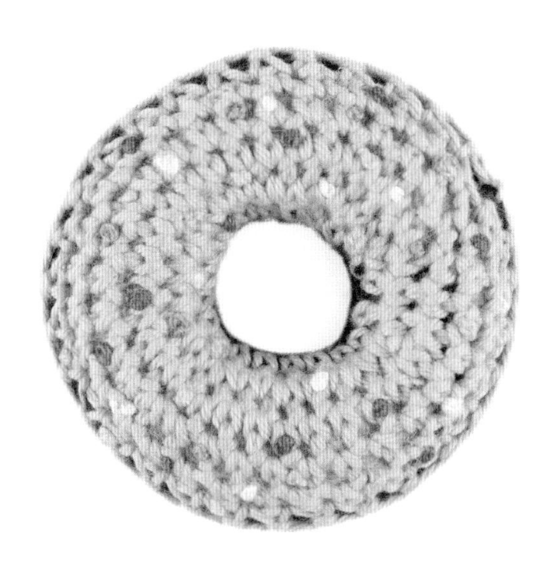

KEY

chain (ch)

slip stitch (sl st)

double crochet (dc)

dc2inc

CHOCOLATE BASE

With 2.5mm hook and A, make 20 ch. Join with a sl st to first ch to form a ring.

Round 1: 1 ch, work 1 dc into each ch (20 sts).

Round 2: 1 dc in each dc.

Round 3 (inc): (Dc2inc, 1 dc) 10 times (30 sts).

Rounds 4–5: 1 dc in each st.

Fasten off.

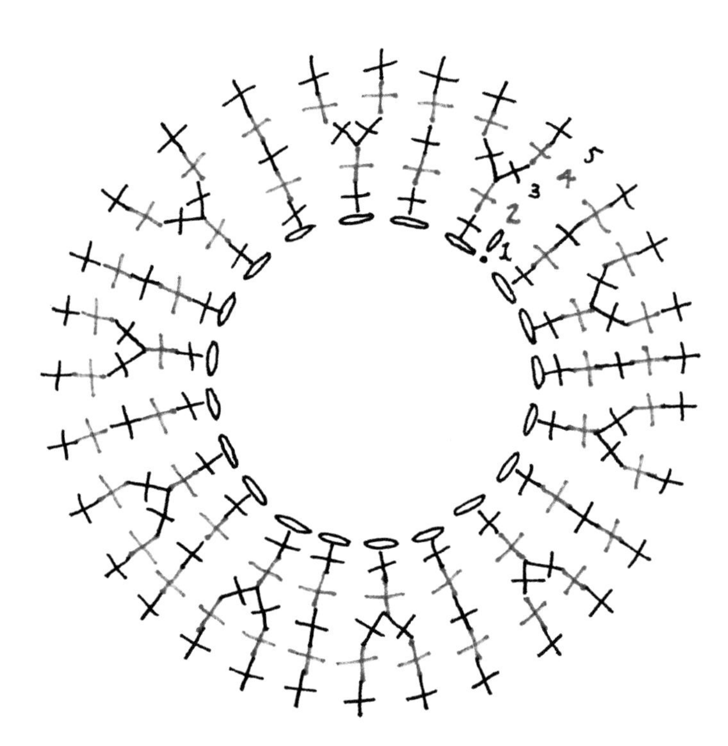

CHOCOLATE BASE

ICING

Round 1: With 2.5mm hook and RS of Base facing, join B with a sl st to the opposite side of the first of the 20 ch sts, 1 dc in same ch as sl st, 1 dc in the opposite side of the next 19 ch (20 sts).

Round 2 (inc): (Dc2inc, 1 dc) 10 times (30 sts).

Rounds 3–4: 1 dc in each st. Do not fasten off.

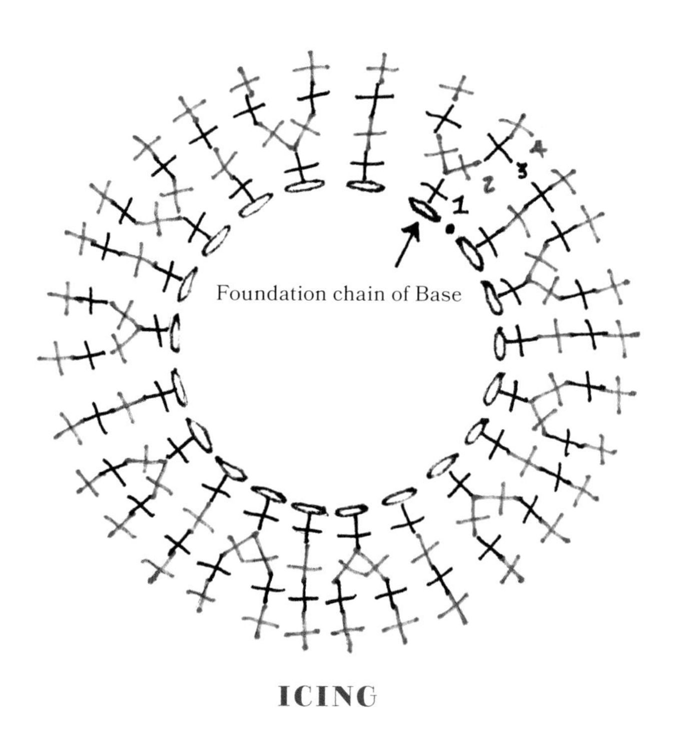

ICING

MAKING UP

With WS together and chocolate base facing, work 1 dc into each dc of the last round of base and icing at the same time to join, stuffing the piece as you go. Embroider a number of French knots (see below) using the oddments of coloured yarns or threads to represent the sugar decorations. Sew the brooch bar to the back of the doughnut.

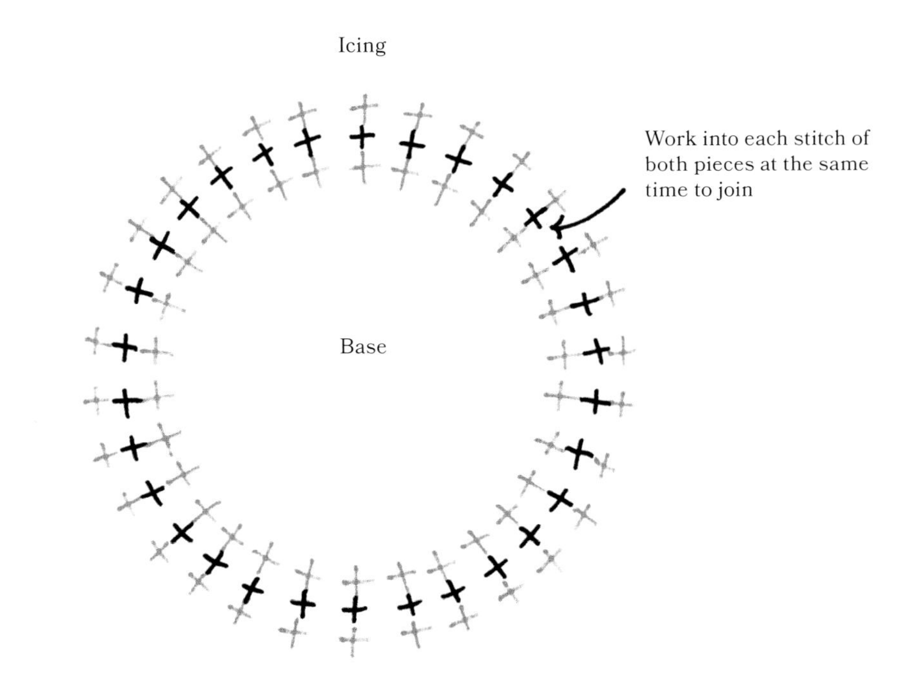

JOIN BASE & ICING

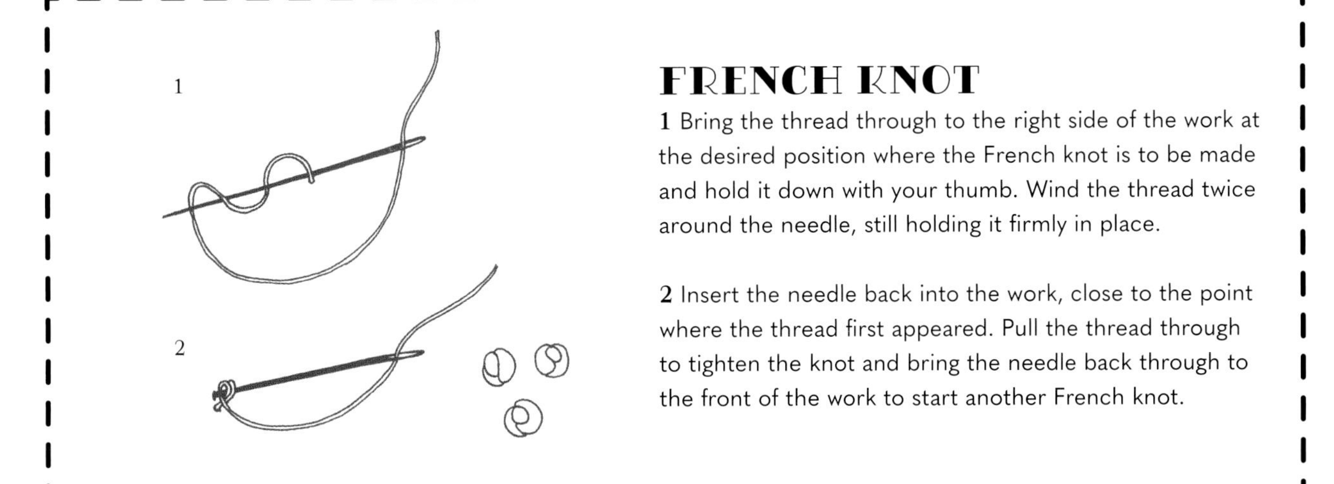

FRENCH KNOT

1 Bring the thread through to the right side of the work at the desired position where the French knot is to be made and hold it down with your thumb. Wind the thread twice around the needle, still holding it firmly in place.

2 Insert the needle back into the work, close to the point where the thread first appeared. Pull the thread through to tighten the knot and bring the needle back through to the front of the work to start another French knot.

PRETTY POSY

Inspired by a collection of vintage porcelain floral brooches, this posy of bright blooms is just as elegant. Delicacy is created in the use of fine cotton and metallic threads.

MATERIALS
- Crochet thread 20 in white (A), yellow (B), blue (C), pink (D) and green (E)
- Embroidery thread in metallic gold, using only two strands worked together (F)
- 0.75mm (UK5:US12) crochet hook
- Sewing needle
- 1in (2.5cm) brooch bar

SIZE
Approximately 2in (5cm) across leafy base

TENSION
52 sts and 50 rows to 4in (10cm) over double crochet using 0.75mm hook and A. Use larger or smaller hook if necessary to obtain correct tension.

NOTES
1 ch at beg of the row/round does not count as a st throughout.

3 ch at beg of round counts as first treble throughout.

METHOD
Each flower is made and finished separately before being arranged on the leafy base. A variety of stitches is used in the pattern, including double crochet, half treble and treble. The gold centres of the periwinkle and daffodil are worked using metallic embroidery thread, but a pretty bead can be stitched in place if preferred.

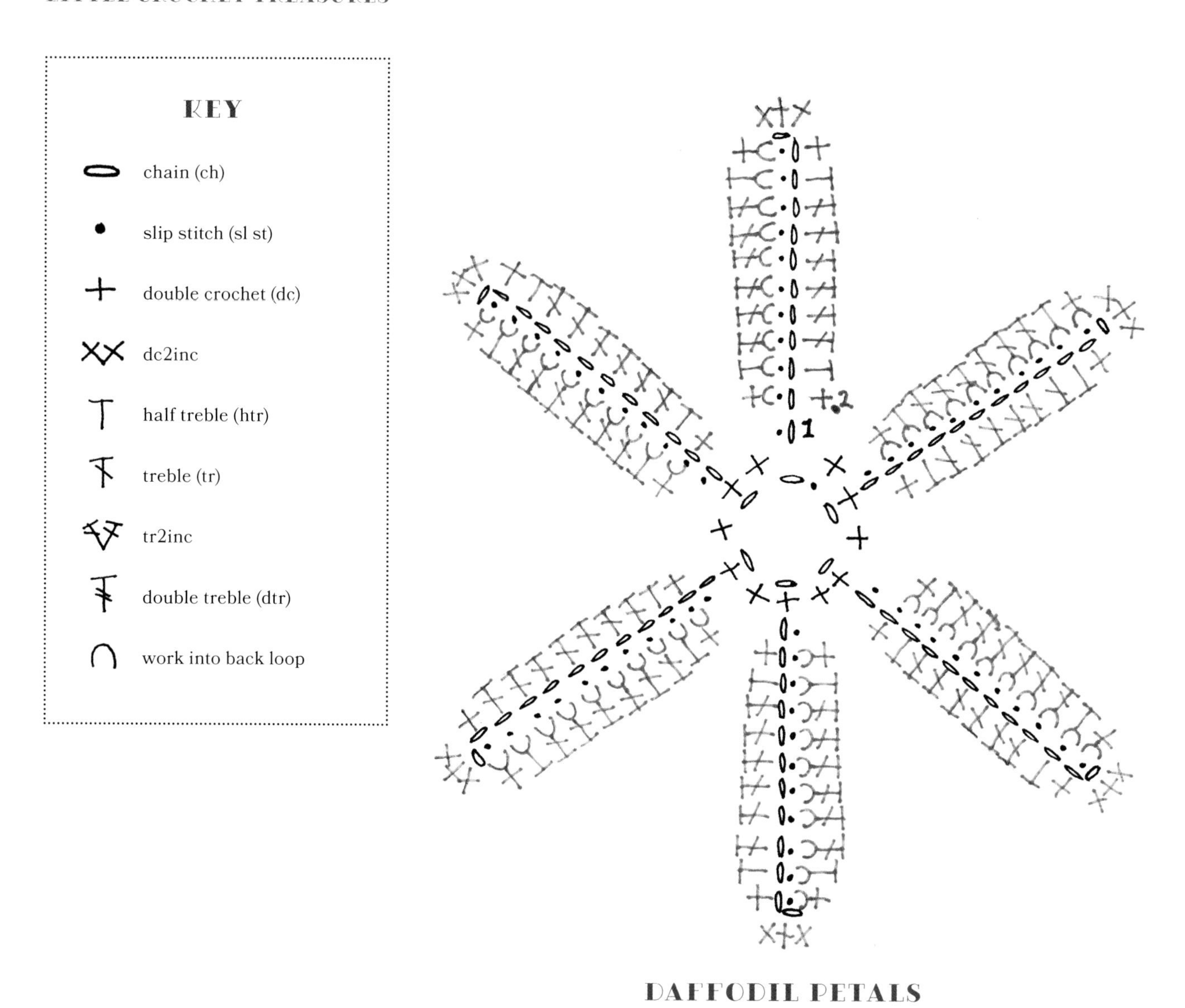

DAFFODIL PETALS

DAFFODIL PETALS

With 0.75mm hook and A, make 6 ch and join with a sl st to first ch to form a ring.

Round 1: (12 ch, sl st in 2nd ch from hook, sl st in next 10 ch, 2 dc into ring) 5 times, 12 ch, sl st in 2nd ch from hook, sl st in next 10 ch, 1 dc into ring (6 spokes).

Round 2: Working into opposite side of each ch, (skip first ch, 1 dc in next ch, 1 htr in next ch, 1 tr in next 6 ch, 1 htr in next ch, 1 dc in next ch, 3 dc in end; working into back loop only of each sl st on other side of petal, 1 dc in first st, 1 htr in next st, 1 tr in next 6 sts, 1 htr in next st, 1 dc in next st, skip next st) 6 times, sl st to first dc (6 petals). Fasten off.

DAFFODIL TRUMPET

With 0.75mm hook and B, leaving a long tail of thread at the beginning, make 4 ch and join with a sl st to first ch to form a ring.
Round 1: 1 ch, 6 dc into ring (6 sts).
Round 2 (inc): (Dc2inc) 6 times (12 sts).
Rounds 3–6: 1 dc in each st.
Round 7 (inc): 3 ch, 1 tr in same st, (tr2inc) 11 times, sl st to 3rd of 3 ch (24 sts).
Fasten off.

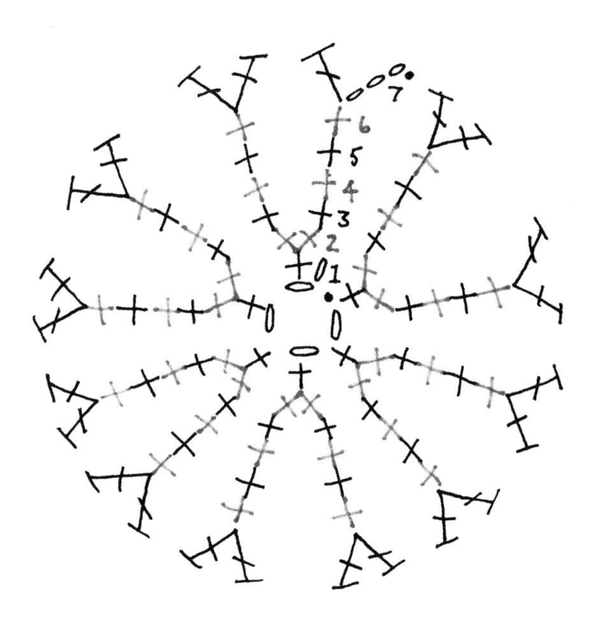

DAFFODIL TRUMPET

DAFFODIL BEAD

DAFFODIL BEAD

With 0.75mm hook and 2 strands of F held together, make 5 ch and join with a sl st to form a ring.
Next: 3 ch, work 15 tr into ring, sl st to 3rd of 3 ch. Fasten off, leaving a long tail of thread. Weave the tail of thread through the tops of the stitches, pull tightly on the thread to close the opening and fasten off, creating a little bead.

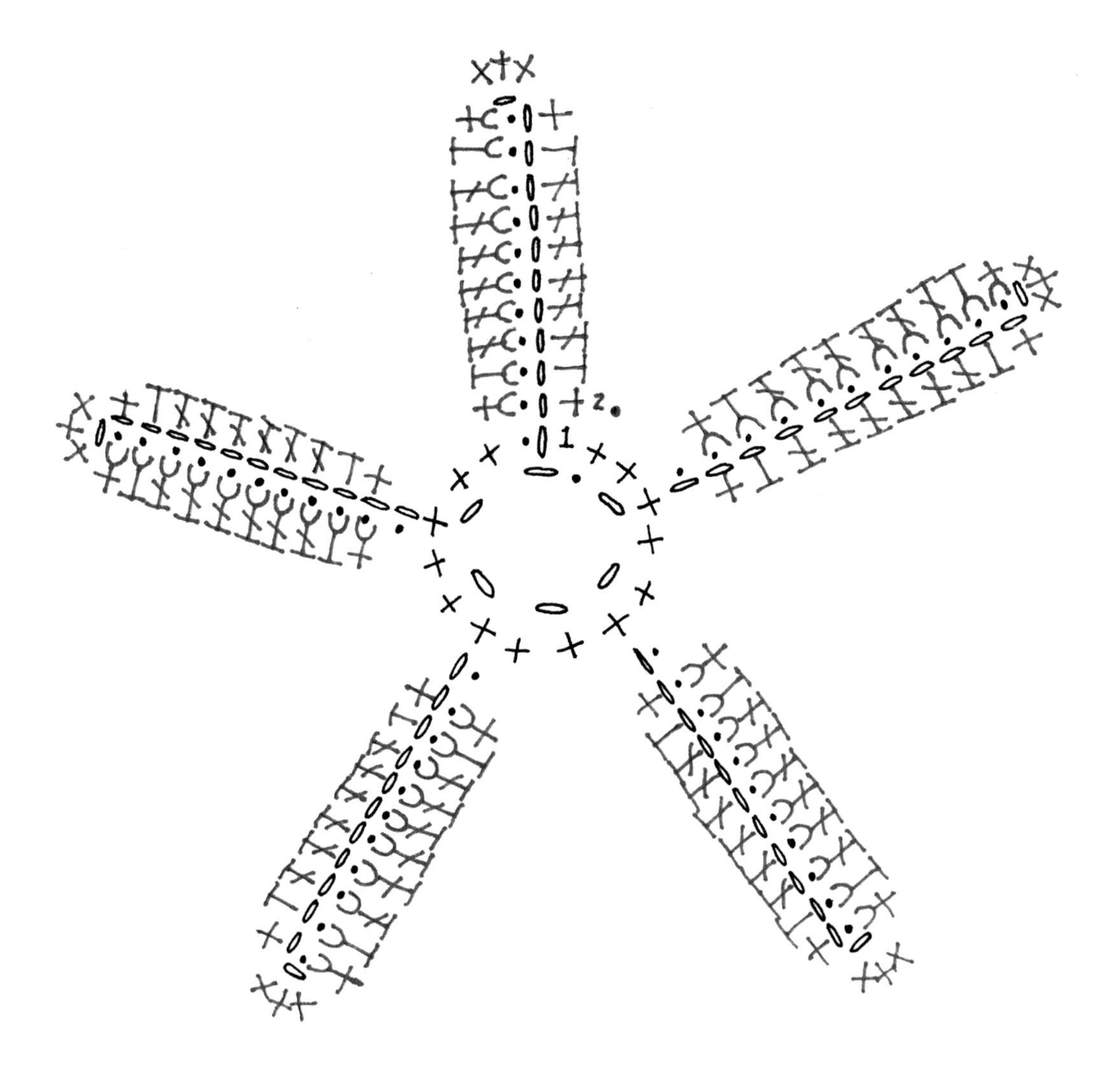

PERIWINKLE

PERIWINKLE PETALS

With 0.75mm hook and B, make 6 ch and join with a sl st to first ch to form a ring.

Round 1: (12 ch, sl st in 2nd ch from hook, sl st in next 10 ch, 3 dc into ring) 4 times, 12 ch, sl st in 2nd ch from hook, sl st in next 10 ch, 2 dc into ring. Join C in last dc (5 spokes).

Round 2: With C, work as given for round 2 of daffodil petals 5 times, sl st to first dc and fasten off (5 petals).

PERIWINKLE BEAD

Work as instructions for Daffodil Bead on page 63.

CHRYSANTHEMUM

With 0.75mm hook and D, make 22 ch, sl st in 2nd ch from hook, sl st in each ch to end, turn, sl st into 2nd and 3rd sts.

Next: (18 ch, sl st in 2nd ch from hook, sl st in next 16 ch, turn, skip first st, sl st in next 2 sts) 19 times (20 petals). Fasten off, leaving a long tail of thread.

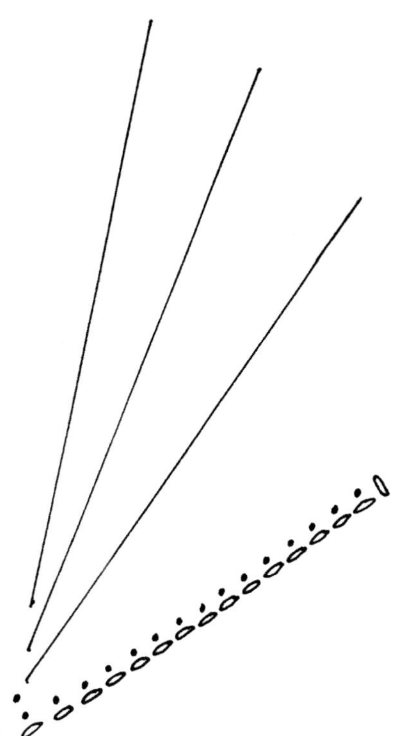

CHRYSANTHEMUM

LEAFY BASE

LEAFY BASE

With 0.75mm hook and E, make 6 ch and join with a sl st to first ch to form a ring.

Round 1: 3 ch, 13 tr into ring, sl st to 3rd of 3 ch (14 sts).

Round 2 (inc): 3 ch, 1 tr in same st as sl st, (tr2inc) 13 times, sl st to 3rd of 3 ch (28 sts).

Round 3: 11 ch, skip 1 tr, (1 dc in next 3 tr, 10 ch, skip 1 tr) 6 times, 1 dc in next 2 tr (7 10-ch sps).

Round 4: (3 dc, 1 htr, 3 tr, 7 dtr, 3 tr, 1 htr, 3 dc) into each 10-ch sp, sl st to first dc. Fasten off.

MAKING UP

Sew the crocheted bead of the daffodil to the inside of the trumpet. Stitch the trumpet to the centre of the petals, using the tail of thread left at the beginning. Sew the other crocheted bead to the centre of the periwinkle petals. Wind the length of the chrysanthemum petals up from the fastened-off end, keeping the base flat and stitching the layers in place with the tail of thread left after fastening off.

Twist the petals to curl. Starting with the periwinkle, sew each bloom to the base, stitching neatly through the petals of the periwinkle and daffodil, and through the base of the chrysanthemum. Weave in all the thread ends. Attach a brooch bar to the back of the leafy base. Sew through each hole on both sides, or around the bar if there are no holes.

VARIATION: SINGLE BLOOM BROOCHES

Make the flowers to wear as a single bloom with a small leafy base to back them. Experiment with different shades of thread for an alternative look.

DAFFODIL LEAFY BASE

With 0.75mm hook and E, make 6 ch and join with a sl st to first ch to form a ring.

Round 1: 3 ch, 11 tr into ring, sl st to 3rd of 3 ch (12 sts).

Round 2: 3 ch, 1 tr in same st as sl st, (tr2inc) 11 times, sl st to 3rd of 3 ch (24 sts).

Round 3: 11 ch, skip first tr, (1 dc in next 3 tr, 10 ch, skip 1 tr) 5 times, 1 dc in next 2 tr (6 10-ch sps).

Round 4: (3 dc, 1 htr, 3 tr, 7 dtr, 3 tr, 1 htr, 3 dc) into each 10-ch sp, sl st to first dc. Fasten off.

Sew the finished flower neatly to the base with the petals positioned in between the leaves. Attach a brooch bar to the back of the leafy base, as for the posy.

DAFFODIL LEAFY BASE

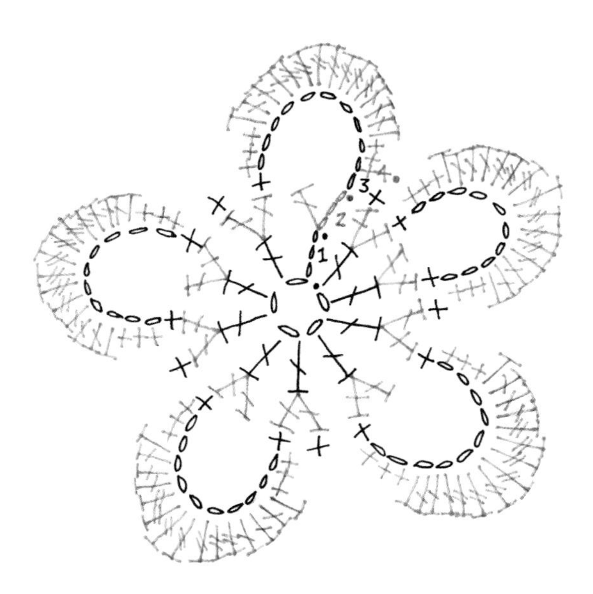

PERIWINKLE AND CHRYSANTHEMUM LEAFY BASE

PERIWINKLE AND CHRYSANTHEMUM LEAFY BASE

With 0.75mm hook and E, make 5 ch and join with a sl st to first ch to form a ring.

Round 1: 3 ch, 9 tr into ring, sl st to 3rd of 3 ch (10 sts).

Round 2: 3 ch, 1 tr in same st as sl st, (tr2inc) 9 times, sl st to 3rd of 3 ch (20 sts).

Round 3: 11 ch, skip 1 tr, (1 dc in next 3 tr, 10 ch, skip 1 tr) 4 times, 1 dc in next 2 tr (5 10-ch sps).

Round 4: (3 dc, 1 htr, 3 tr, 7 dtr, 3 tr, 1 htr, 3 dc) into each 10-ch sp, sl st to first dc. Fasten off.

Attach the periwinkle as for daffodil. Sew the chrysanthemum to the base and twist the petals to curl into shape. Attach a brooch bar to the back of the leafy base, as for the posy.

DELICATE POPPY

By using a fine thread, the petals of this dainty crocheted poppy brooch will feel almost as delicate as the real thing. A thicker thread will produce a more compact, sturdier fabric.

MATERIALS

- Crochet thread 20 in black (A), yellow (with optional lime-green metallic machine embroidery thread worked together) (B)
- Crochet thread 40 or 20 in red or pink (C)
- 0.75mm (UK5:US12) crochet hook
- Tiny amount of toy stuffing
- Sewing needle
- 1in (2.5cm) brooch bar

SIZE

Approximately 2½in (6.5cm) across

TENSION

52 sts and 50 rows to 4in (10cm) over double crochet using 0.75mm hook and crochet thread 20.

56 sts and 52 rows to 4in (10cm) over double crochet using 0.75mm hook and crochet thread 40.

Use larger or smaller hook if necessary to obtain correct tension.

NOTES

1 ch at beg of the round does not count as a st throughout.

3 ch at beg of the round counts as a st throughout.

METHOD

A similar pattern to the Giant Poppy (see pages 106–111), this delicate version uses the long crochet stitchcs and very fine thread to form the papery quality of poppy petals. The yellow centre is filled with a tiny amount of stuffing, and the black cotton thread surrounding it is folded back on itself and stitched in place.

KEY

- chain (ch)
- slip stitch (sl st)
- double crochet (dc)
- half treble (htr)
- treble (tr)
- tr2inc
- double treble (dtr)
- dtr2inc
- dtr3inc
- direction of work

POPPY CENTRE

With 0.75mm hook and A, make 4 ch and join with a sl st to the first ch to form a ring.

Round 1: 3 ch, 10 tr into ring, sl st to 3rd of 3 ch with B and carry A on WS of work (11 sts).

Rounds 2–3: 3 ch, 1 tr in next 10 tr, sl st to 3rd of 3 ch.

Continue with A.

Round 4 (inc): 3 ch, 1 tr in same st, (tr2inc) 10 times, sl st to 3rd of 3 ch (22 sts).

Rounds 5–9: 3 ch, (to count as first tr), 1 tr in each tr, sl st to 3rd of 3 ch.

Fasten off, leaving a long tail of A and B. Stuff the yellow-green centre piece. Weave the tail of B around the lower edges of the centre piece, between rounds 3 and 4, pull tightly on the thread to gather the stitches and fasten off.

Weave the tail of A through the last round of stitches, pull tightly on the thread to close the opening and fasten off. Push the yellow centre inside the surrounding black section. Sew the sections in place, working the stitches right through from the base to the top of the yellow centre. Pliers may come in handy here to help coax the needle through the stuffed piece.

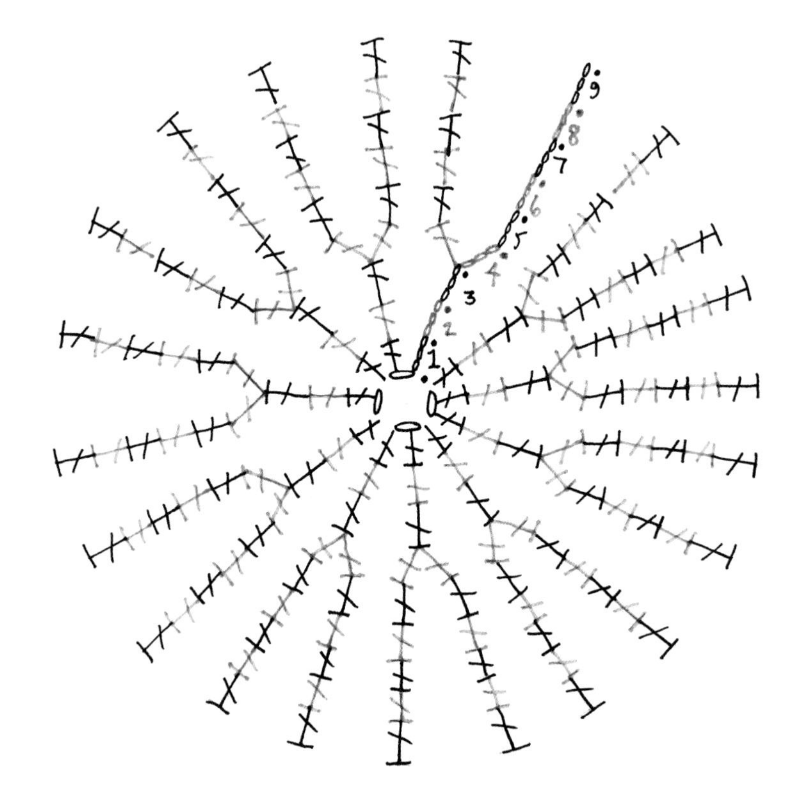

POPPY CENTRE

POPPY PETALS

With 0.75mm hook and A, make 6 ch and join with a sl st to form a ring.

Round 1 (RS): 3 ch, 2 tr into ring, (9 ch, 3 tr) 3 times, 9 ch, sl st to 3rd of 3 ch (12 tr and 4 9-ch sps).

Round 2: *Skip next tr, 1 dc into next tr, skip next tr, (4 dc, 2 htr, 2 tr, 5 dtr, 2 tr, 2 htr, 4 dc) into next 9-ch sp*; rep from * to * 3 more times, sl st to first dc.

Sl st in next 4 dc of first petal. Join C in last sl st.

Continue with C.

Round 3: *1 htr in next 2 htr, 1 tr in next tr, (dtr3inc, dtr2inc) 3 times, dtr3inc, 1 tr in next tr, 1 htr in next 2 htr, skip next 4 dc down side of petal, skip dc in between petals, skip next 4 dc of next petal*; rep from * to * 3 more times (96 sts).

Round 4 (inc): (1 htr in next 2 htr, 1 tr in next tr, dtr2inc in next 18 sts, 1 tr in next tr, 1 htr in next 2 htr) 4 times, sl st to first htr of next petal, turn (168 sts).

Round 5 (WS) (inc): Working on the WS of the petals, (skip next htr, 1 htr in next htr, 1 tr in next tr, dtr2inc in next 36 sts, 1 tr in next tr, 1 htr in next htr, skip next htr) 4 times, sl st to first htr. Fasten off (304 sts).

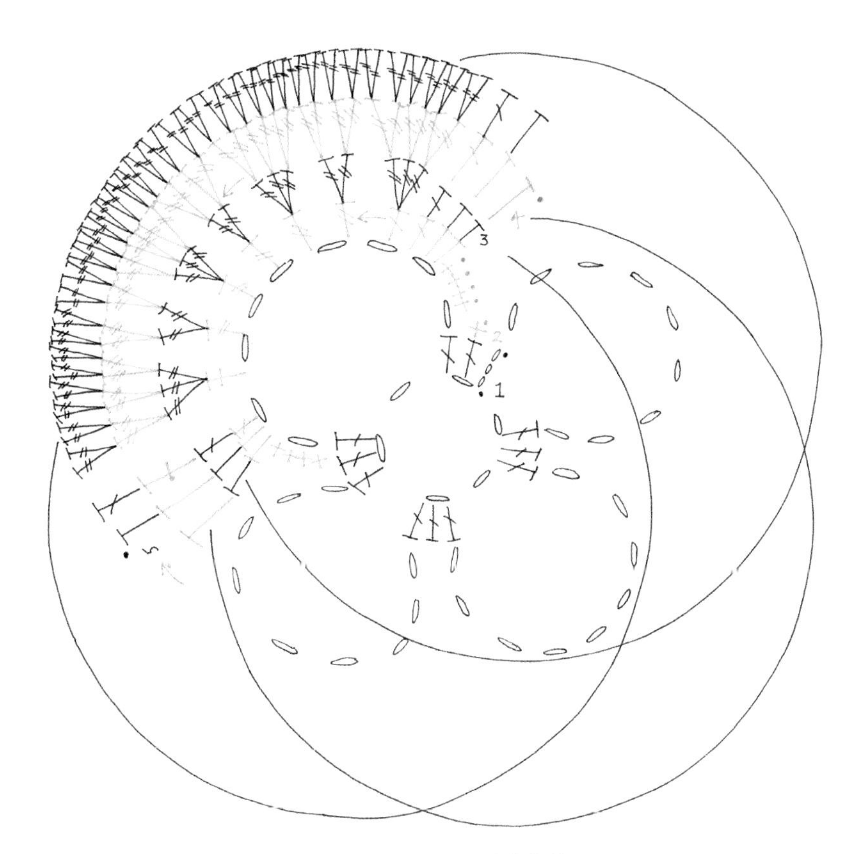

POPPY PETALS

MAKING UP

Attach the poppy centre to the middle of the petals on the RS. Weave in all the thread ends. Sew a brooch bar to the back.

NECKLACES

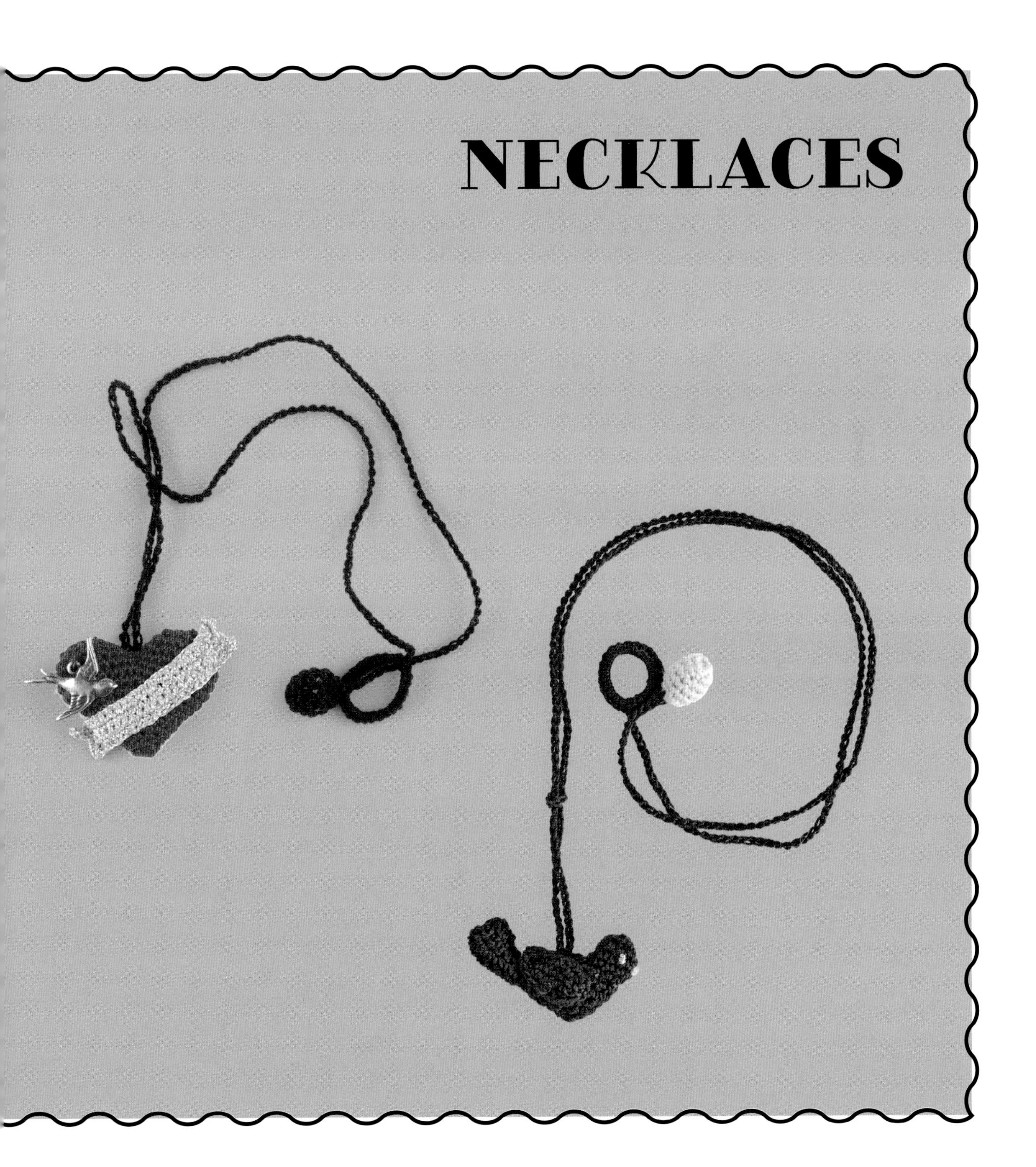

BLACKBIRD

The blackbird, with his golden beak and mellow song, is the inspiration for this delicate crocheted necklace, fastened with a tiny egg.

MATERIALS

- Crochet thread 20 in black (A)
- Stranded embroidery thread in blue-green for the egg, and silver and yellow for the eyes and beak
- 0.75mm (UK5:US12) crochet hook
- Tiny amount of toy stuffing
- Sewing needle

SIZE

Approximately 1¼in (3cm) from beak to tip of tail

TENSION

52 sts and 50 rows to 4in (10cm) over double crochet using 0.75mm hook and A.
Use larger or smaller hook if necessary to obtain correct tension.

NOTE
1 ch and 2 ch at beg of the row/round does not count as a st throughout.

METHOD

The blackbird body is like that of the Fantail Dove pattern (see pages 150–153), but uses a smaller hook and fine thread to create the tiny, delicate stitches. The wings and tail are made separately and attached to the body, along with a loop from which to hang the bird on the crocheted chain necklace. A loop at one end and a little bird egg button at the other fastens the chain.

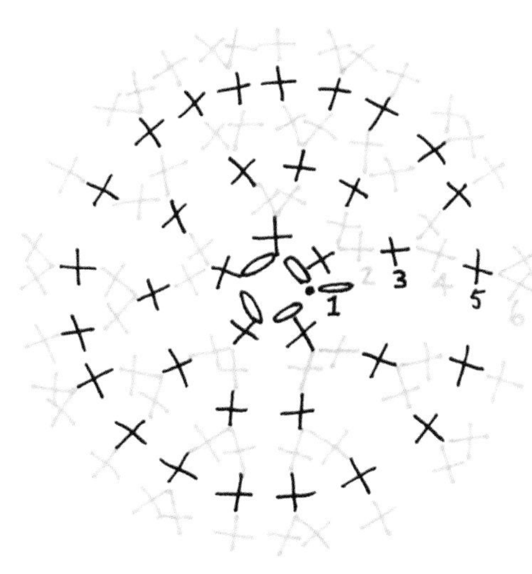

BODY ROUNDS 1–6

KEY

- chain (ch)
- slip stitch (sl st)
- double crochet (dc)
- dc2inc
- half treble (htr)
- treble (tr)
- slip stitch together back loops on each side to join

BODY

With 0.75mm hook and A, make 4 ch and join with a sl st to the first ch to form a ring.

Round 1: 1 ch, 5 dc into ring (5 sts).

Round 2 (inc): (Dc2inc) 5 times (10 sts).

Round 3: 1 dc in each st.

Round 4 (inc): (Dc2inc) 10 times (20 sts).

Round 5: 1 dc in each st.

Round 6 (inc): (Dc2inc, 1 dc) 10 times (30 sts).

Round 7: Fold piece and sl st together the back loops of the next 10 sts on each side to join the back of the bird, leaving the remaining 10 sts for the shaping of the head. Work 1 dc in each of the remaining 10 sts.

Shape head

Rounds 8–9: 1 dc in each dc.

Fasten off, leaving a long tail of thread. Stuff the bird with a tiny amount of toy stuffing. Weave the tail of thread through the last round of stitches, pull tightly on the thread to close the opening and fasten off.

With A, sew a row of stitches below the start of the head shaping and pull on the thread, but not too tightly, to indicate the neck. Fasten off.

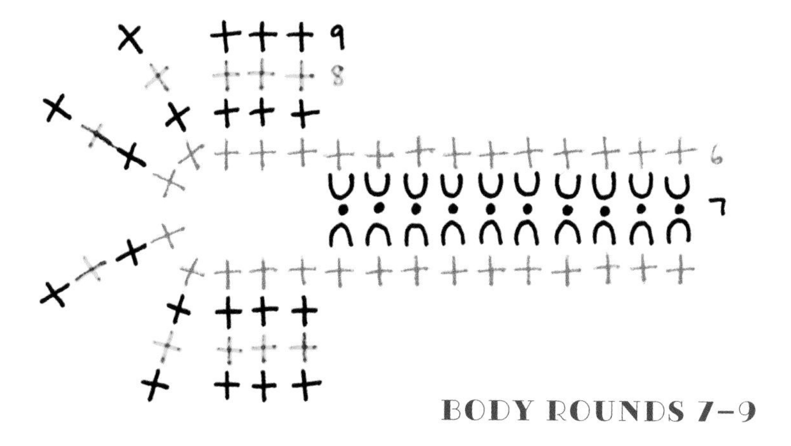

BODY ROUNDS 7–9

WING (MAKE 2)

With 0.75mm hook and A, make 8 ch.

Round 1: 1 dc into 2nd ch from hook, 1 dc in next 5 ch, 3 dc in end ch, 1 dc down opposite side of each chain to end (15 sts).

Round 2: 2 ch, 1 dc in next 3 dc, 1 htr in next dc, 1 tr in next dc, 1 htr in next dc, 1 dc in next dc, sl st to next st, fasten off.

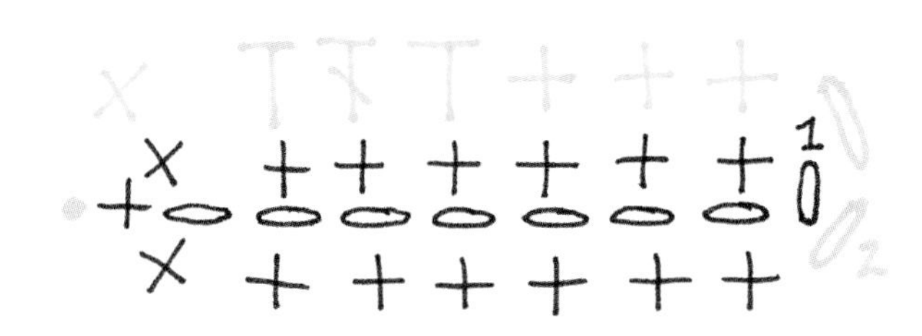

WING

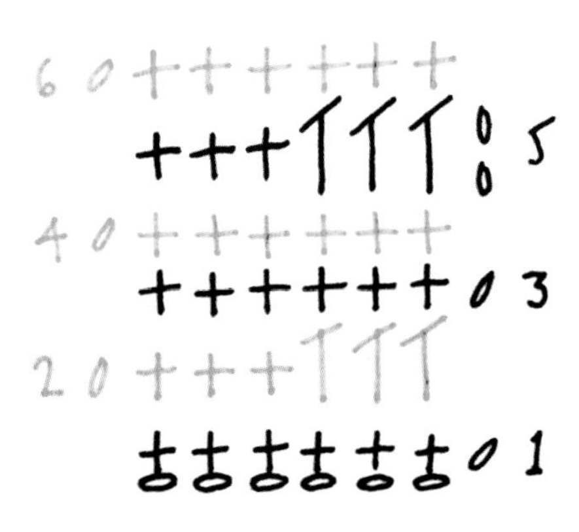

TAIL ROWS 1–6

TAIL

With 0.75mm hook and A, make 7 ch.

Row 1: 1 dc into 2nd ch from hook, 1 dc into next 5 ch, turn (6 sts).

Row 2: 1 ch, 1 dc in next 3 dc, 1 htr in next 3 dc, turn.

Row 3: 1 ch, 1 dc in next 6 sts, turn.

Row 4: As row 3.

Row 5: 2 ch, 1 htr in next 3 sts, 1 dc in the next 3 sts, turn.

Row 6: 1 ch, 1 dc in next 6 sts, turn.

Row 7: Fold the piece lengthways, (1 ch, sl st tog the back loops only of next 2 sts down edge of tail) 3 times. Fasten off.

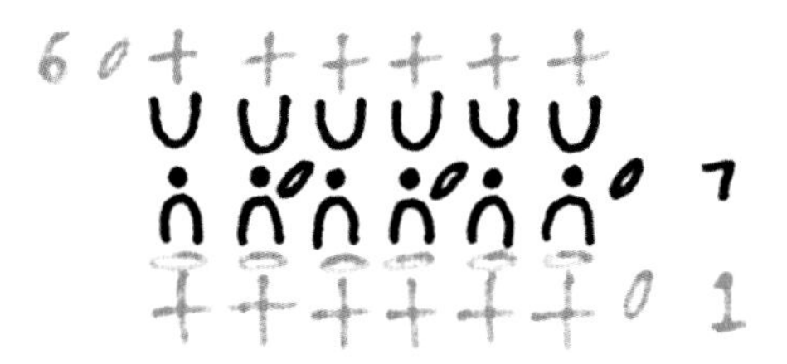

TAIL ROW 7

NECKLACE

Egg

With 0.75mm hook and 3 strands of embroidery thread held together, make 4 ch and join with a sl st to first ch to form a ring.

Round 1: 1 ch, 6 dc into ring.

Round 2 (inc): (Dc2inc) 6 times (12 sts).

Rounds 3–6: 1 dc in each st.

Fasten off, leaving a long tail of thread. Stuff the egg firmly. Weave the tail of thread through the last round of stitches, pull tightly on the thread to close the opening and fasten off.

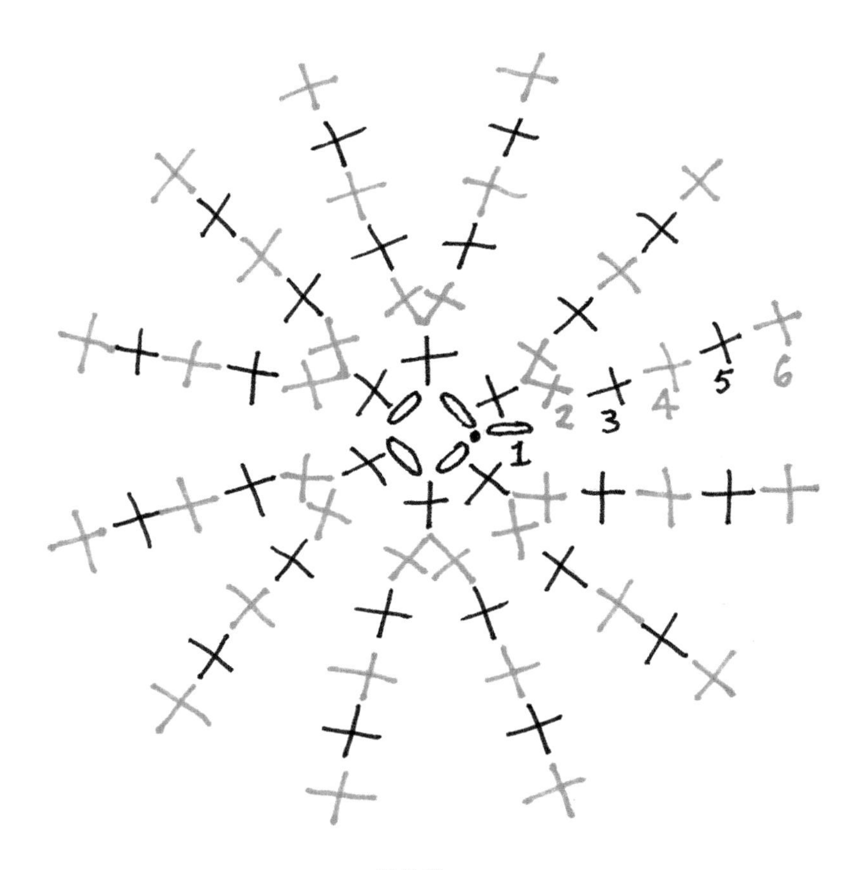

EGG

Chain and loop

With 0.75mm hook and A, make 16 ch and join with sl st to form a ring.
1 ch, 24 dc into ring, sl st to first dc.
Next: Work a chain measuring 16in (41cm), or to desired length.
Fasten off, leaving a tail of thread to stitch the finished chain securely to the gathered end of the egg. Weave in ends.

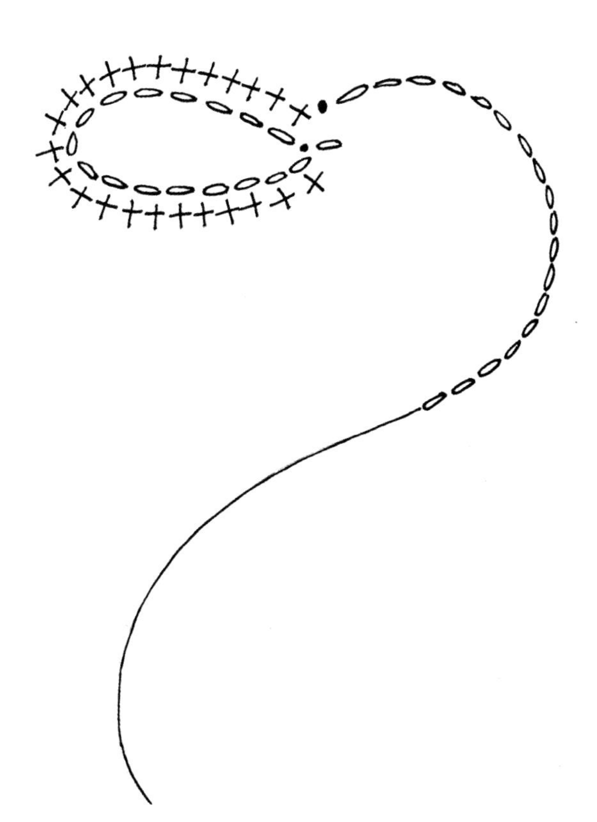

CHAIN AND LOOP

MAKING UP

Sew the narrow end of the tail to the bird. Join the wings to the sides of the body. Using one strand of silver and yellow thread, embroider the eyes and beak. Using 0.75mm hook and A, make 40 ch, join with a sl st to first ch to form a loop. Fasten off and stitch to the centre back of the bird. Weave in any loose ends. Attach the blackbird to the chain by looping the loop on the back of the bird over the chain of the necklace, and then thread the blackbird through the loop.

LOVE HEART TATTOO

This delicate necklace captures the symbolism of love and protection within the tattoo tradition. Adorned with a simple charm, it will make a treasured keepsake.

MATERIALS

- Crochet thread 20 in red (A) and black (C)
- Embroidery thread in silver, using only 2 strands worked together (B)
- 0.75mm (UK5:US12) crochet hook
- Small amount of toy stuffing
- Sewing needle
- Swallow charm

FOR BROOCH VARIATION

¾in (2cm) brooch bar

SIZE

Widest part measures approximately 1¼in (3cm)
Longest part measures approximately ⅞in (2.25cm)

TENSION

52 sts and 50 rows to 4in (10cm) over double crochet using 0.75mm hook and A.
Use larger or smaller hook if necessary to obtain correct tension.

METHOD

The heart and ribbon are made in a similar way to the Sweetheart Tattoo (see pages 42–47). However, by using a smaller hook and thread, this finished piece is more delicate and fine-looking. The heart is decorated with a swallow charm, stitched in place, before attaching the pendant to the crocheted chain.

NOTE
1 ch at beg of the row/round does not count as a st throughout.

HEART

With 0.75mm hook and A, make 4 ch and join with a sl st to the first ch to form a ring.
Round 1: 1 ch, 5 dc into ring (5 sts).
Round 2 (inc): (Dc2inc) 5 times (10 sts).
Round 3: 1 dc in each st.
Round 4 (inc): (Dc2inc) 10 times (20 sts).
Rounds 5–6: 1 dc in each st.
Round 7 (inc): (Dc2inc, 1 dc) 10 times (30 sts).
Round 8: 1 dc in each st.
Round 9 (inc): (Dc2inc, 2 dc) 10 times (40 sts).
Rounds 10–11: 1 dc in each st.

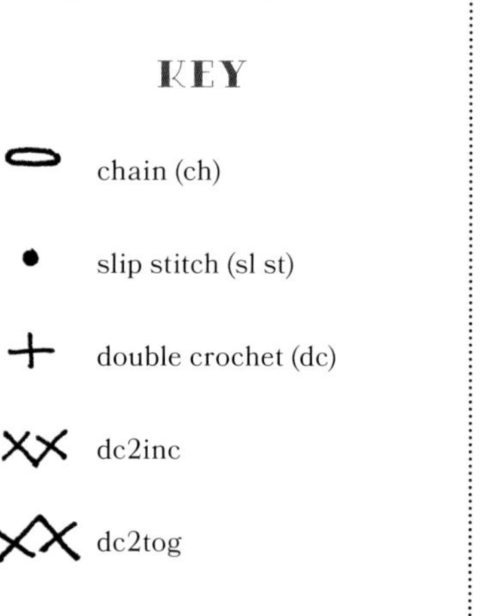

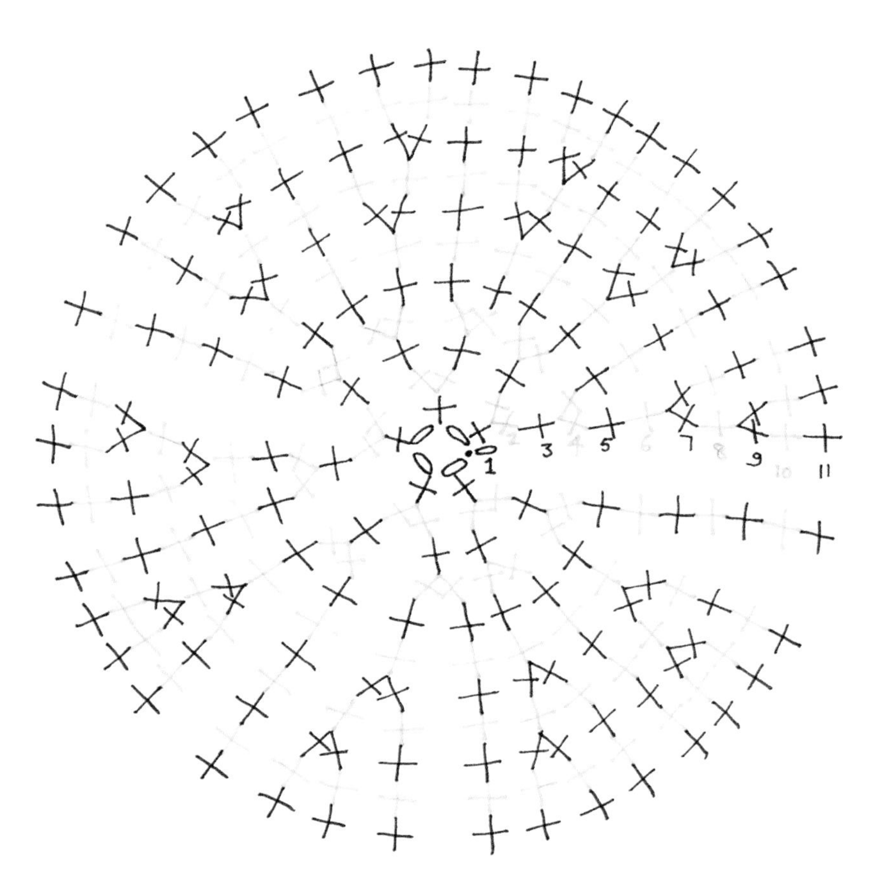

HEART ROUNDS 1–11

Shape top

Round 12: 1 dc in next 10 dc, skip next 20 dc, 1 dc in next 10 dc. Continue on these 20 sts.

Round 13: 1 dc in each st.

Round 14 (dec): (Dc2tog, 2 dc) 5 times (15 sts).

Fasten off, leaving a long tail of thread.

With RS facing, join A with a sl st to the first of the unworked 20 sts. Starting in the same dc as the sl st, work 3 rounds of 1 dc in each st to match first side. Fasten off leaving a long tail of thread.

Stuff the heart firmly. On each side, weave the tail of thread through the last round of stitches. Pull tightly on the thread to close the opening and fasten off. Weave in all the ends.

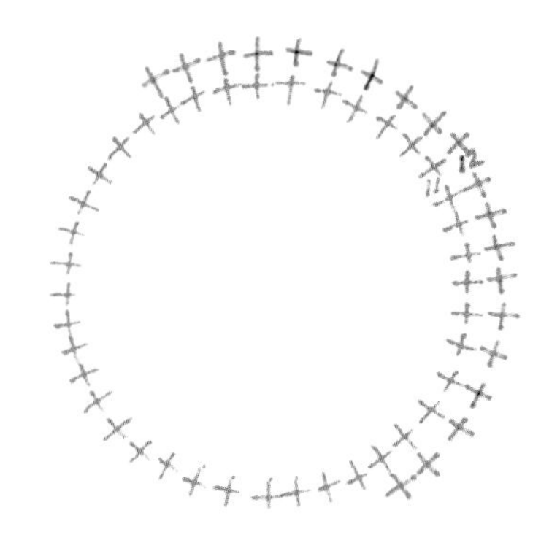

SHAPE TOP ROUND 12

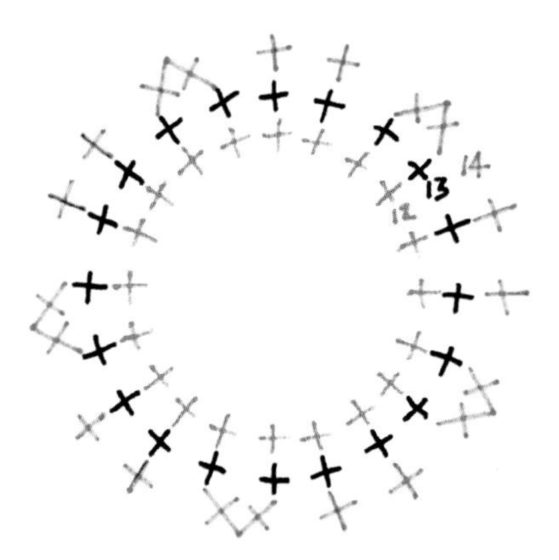

SHAPE TOP ROUNDS 13–14

RIBBON

With 0.75mm hook and B, make 30 ch.

Row 1 (dec): 1 dc into 3rd ch from hook, 1 dc in next 25 ch, dc2tog, turn (27 sts).

Row 2 (dec): Skip the first dc, 1 dc in next 24 dc, dc2tog, turn (25 sts).

Row 3 (inc): 3 ch, 1 dc in 2nd and 3rd ch from hook, 1 dc in next 25 dc, turn (27 sts).

Row 4 (inc): 3 ch, 1 dc into 2nd and 3rd ch from hook, 1 dc in next 26 sts, sl st into next st (29 sts).

Fasten off.

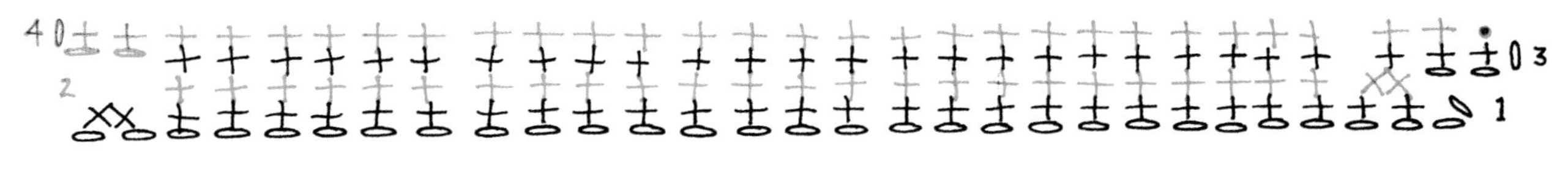

RIBBON

NECKLACE

Link

With 0.75mm hook and A, make 10 ch, join with a sl st to first ch to form a ring. Into the ring work 14 dc, sl st to first dc and fasten off, leaving a long tail of thread.

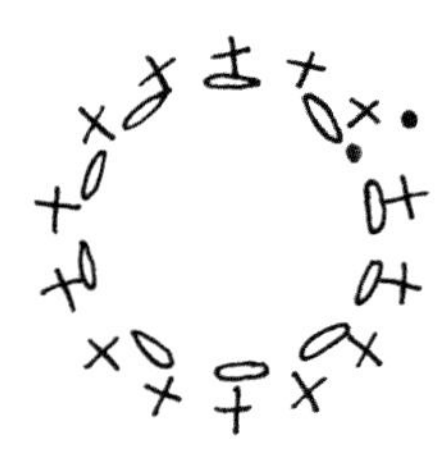

LINK

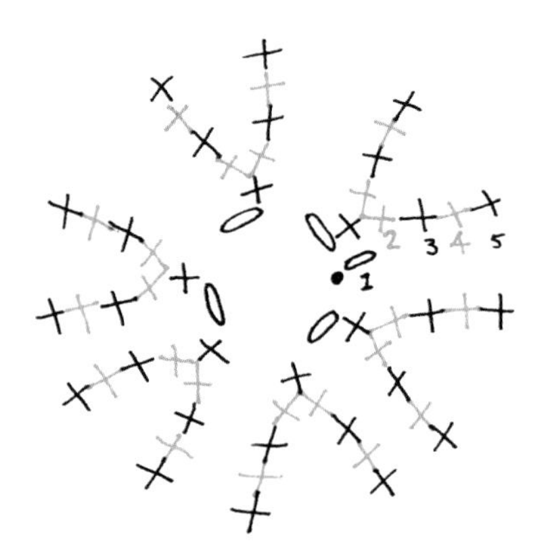

BUTTON

Button

With 0.75mm hook and C, make 4 ch and join with sl st to first ch to form a ring.

Round 1: 1 ch, 6 dc into ring (6 sts).

Round 2 (inc): (Dc2inc) 6 times (12 sts).

Rounds 3–5: 1 dc in each st.

Fasten off, leaving a long tail of thread. Stuff the button firmly. Weave the tail of thread through the last round of stitches, pull up tightly on the thread to close the opening and fasten off.

Chain and loop

With 0.75mm hook and C, make 16 ch and join with sl st to first ch to form a ring.

1 ch, 24 dc into ring, sl st to first dc.

Next: Work a chain measuring 17in (43cm), or to desired length, allowing an extra ⅝in (1.5cm) for attaching the heart. Fasten off and sew the button to the end of the chain.

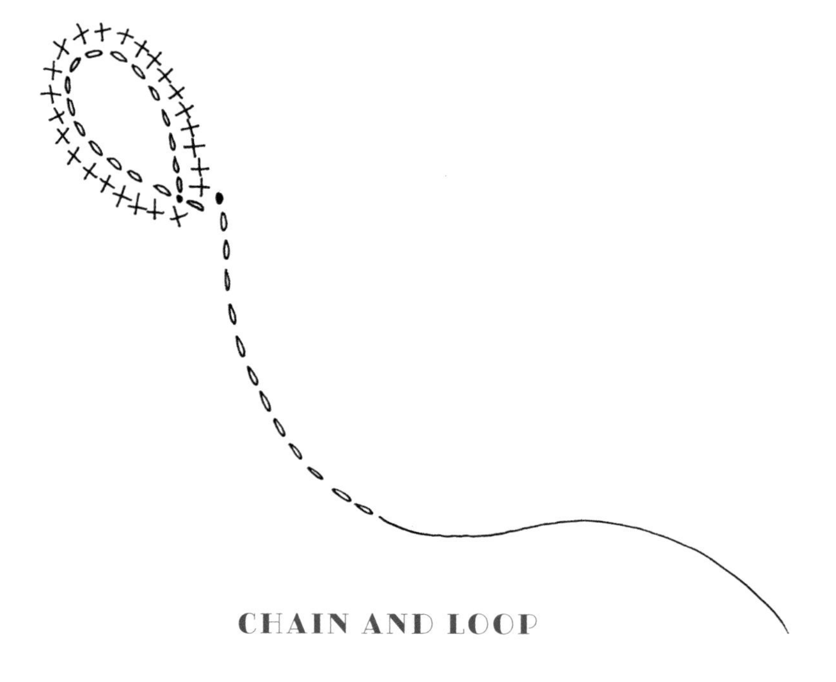

CHAIN AND LOOP

MAKING UP

Position the ribbon at an angle across the heart. Sew in place. The stiff nature of the metallic thread means that it keeps its shape quite well, though the ends can be painted with a little PVA glue to stiffen them, if desired. Stitch the swallow charm to the top shaping at the front, above the lower end of the ribbon. Make the stitch that holds the swallow a little loose to allow the bird to move. With the tail of thread left after fastening off, sew the link just below the top shaping at the back, laying it flat against the heart and leaving a gap at the top of the link to thread the chain through. Fold the chain in the middle to form a loop and thread it through the link, using a crochet hook to catch it and draw it through. Pass the ends of the chain through the loop. Pull on the ends to tighten the loop.

VARIATION: BROOCH

Make the Love Heart Tattoo in the same way, leaving out the link and necklace. Attach a brooch bar to the back of the heart, just below the shaping, at the widest part. Sew through each hole on both sides, or around the bar if there are no holes.

CHERRIES

Full of the vibrancy of summer, the vintage fashion cherry icon is here used to stylish effect as a necklace, blending simple stitches to form a delicate delight.

MATERIALS

- Crochet thread 20 in red (A) and green (B)
- 0.75mm (UK5:US12) crochet hook
- Tiny amount of toy stuffing
- Sewing needle

FOR BROOCH VARIATION

- DK yarn in red (A) and green (B)
- 2.5mm hook
- 1in (2.5cm) brooch bar

SIZE

Approximately 1in (2.5cm) from tops of leaves to base of cherries

TENSION

52 sts and 50 rows to 4in (10cm) over double crochet using 0.75mm hook and A.
Use larger or smaller hook if necessary to obtain correct tension.

METHOD

The fruit is crocheted in continuous rounds. The leaves are worked in rounds using double crochet, half treble and treble stitches to form the shape. After stuffing the cherries, they are attached to the leaves with stalks worked in chain stitch.

NOTE
1 ch at beg of the round does not count as a st throughout.

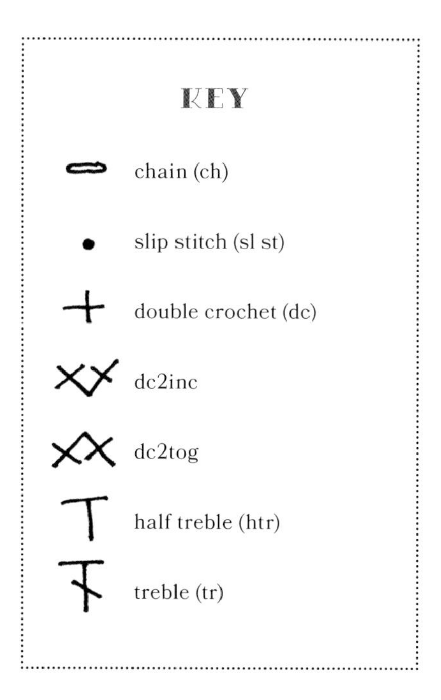

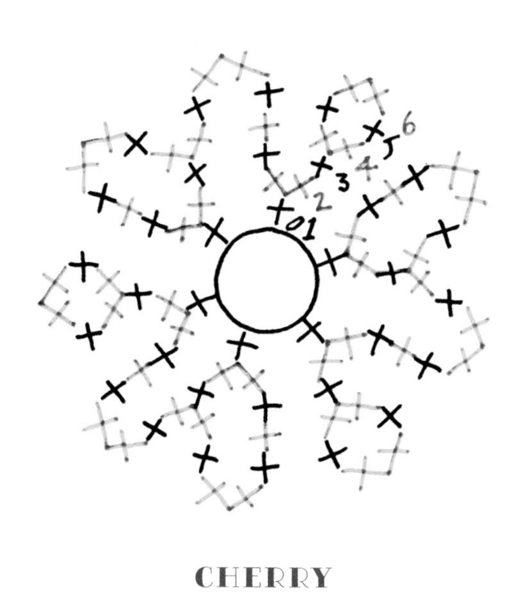

CHERRY

CHERRY (MAKE 2)

With 0.75mm hook and A, make a magic loop.
Round 1: 1 ch, 6 dc into loop (6 sts).
Round 2 (inc): (Dc2inc) 6 times (12 sts).
Round 3: 1 dc in each st. Pull tightly on the short end of thread to close the loop.
Round 4 (inc): (Dc2inc, 1 dc) 6 times (18 sts).
Round 5: 1 dc in each st.
Round 6 (dec): (Dc2tog) 9 times (9 sts).
Fasten off, leaving a long tail of thread. Stuff the cherry and weave the tail of thread through the last round. Pull tightly on the thread to close the opening and fasten off.

LEAF (MAKE 2)

With 0.75mm hook and B make 6 ch.
Round 1: 1 dc into 2nd ch from hook, 1 dc in next 3 ch, 3 dc in next ch, 1 dc down the opposite side of each ch (11 sts).
Round 2: 2 ch, 1 dc in each dc, sl st into 2-ch sp. Fasten off and weave in the ends.

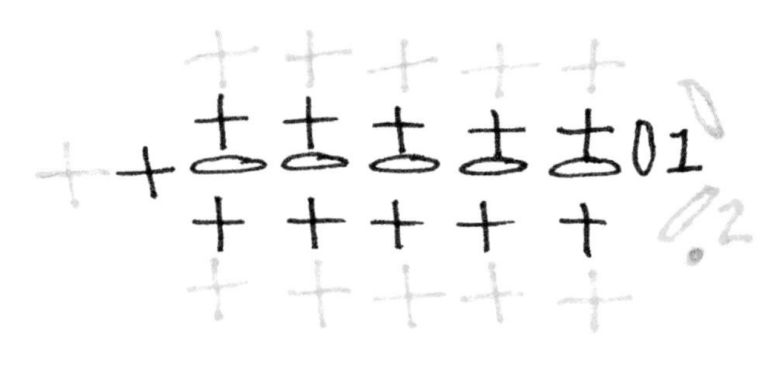

LEAF

STALKS

With 0.75mm hook and B, work 1 dc into the top, gathered end of a cherry, 4 ch, with RS facing work 1 dc into the 2-ch sp of each leaf, 4 ch, 1 dc into the top of the remaining cherry. Fasten off and weave in the ends.

LOOP

With 0.75mm hook and B, make 10 ch and join with a sl st to first ch to form a loop. Stitch securely between the two leaves so the loop faces forward.

Make a chain and fastening as given for the Wild Strawberry necklace (see pages 92–97) and attach the finished cherries.

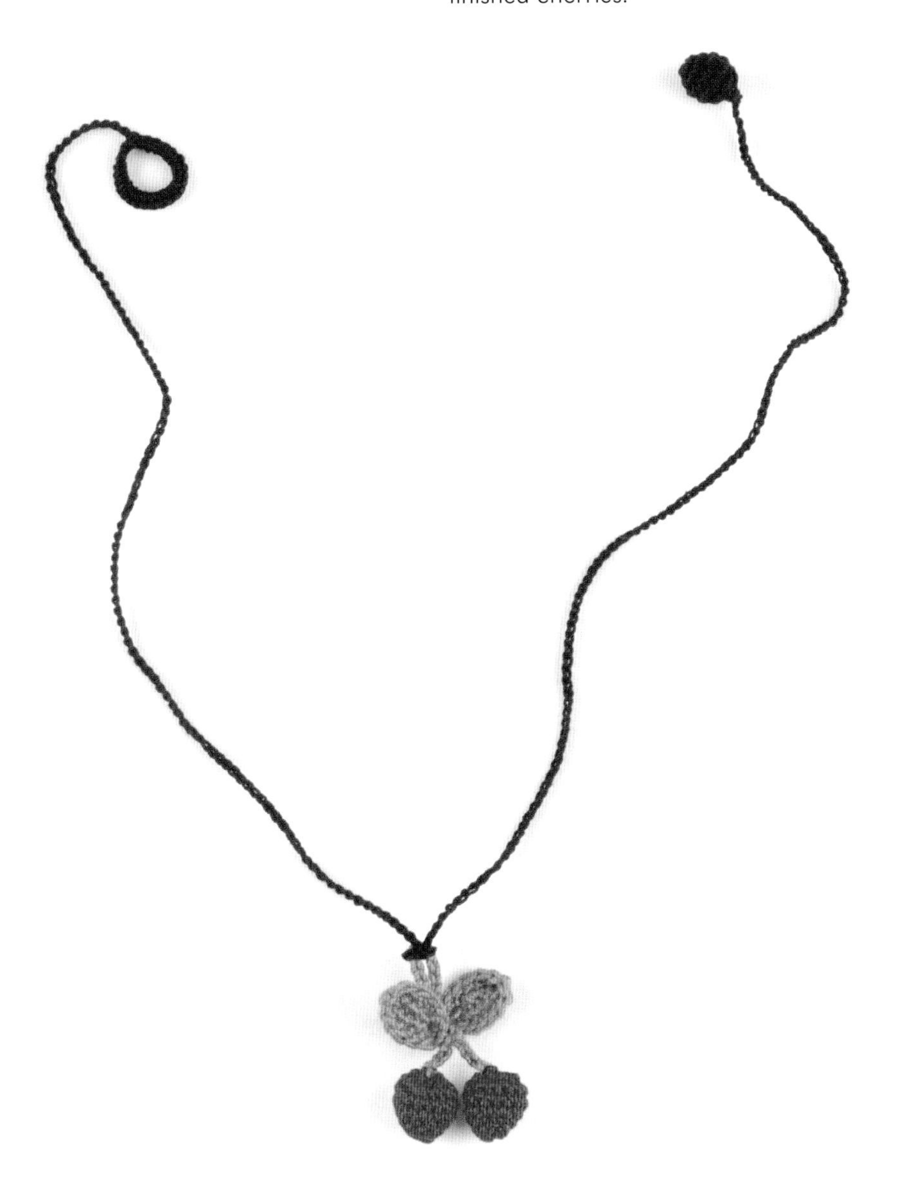

VARIATION: BROOCH

SIZE

Approximately 2¾in (7cm) from tops of leaves to base of cherries

CHERRY (MAKE 2)

Using 2.5mm hook and A, work rounds 1–3 as for the Cherry Necklace.

Round 4 (inc): (Dc2inc) 12 times (24 sts).

Round 5: 1 dc in each st.

Round 6 (dec): (Dc2tog) 12 times (12 sts).

Round 7 (dec): (Dc2tog, 1 dc) 4 times (8 sts).

Fasten off, leaving a long tail of yarn and finish as for the Cherry Necklace.

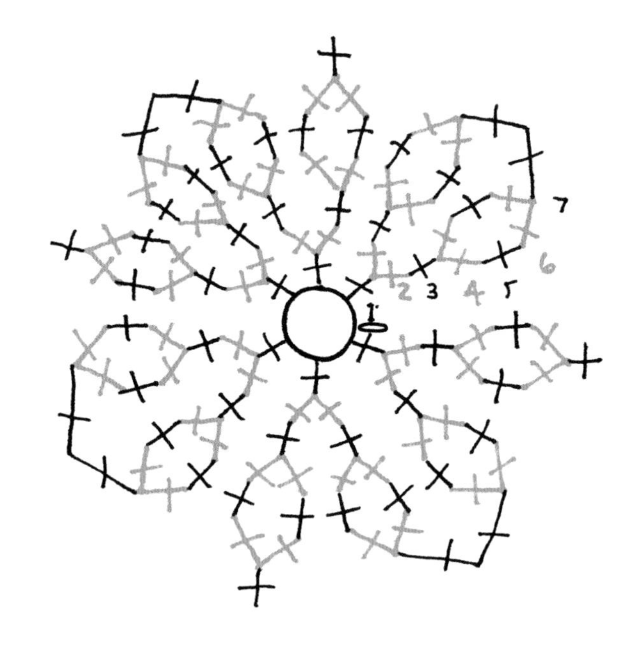

CHERRY

LEAF (MAKE 2)

With 2.5mm hook and B, make 8 ch.

Round 1: 1 dc into 2nd ch from hook, 1 dc in next 5 ch, 3 dc in next ch, 1 dc down opposite side of each ch (15 sts).

Round 2: 3 ch, *1 dc in next dc, 1 htr in next dc, 1 tr in next 3 dc, 1 htr in next dc*, 1 dc in next 2 dc; rep from * to *, 1 dc in next dc, sl st into 3-ch sp. Fasten off and weave in the ends.

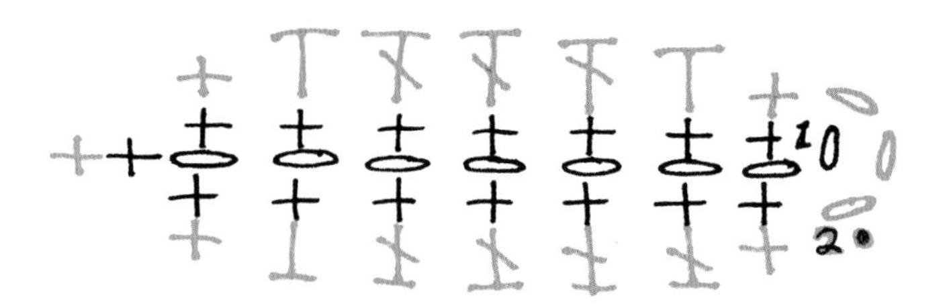

LEAF

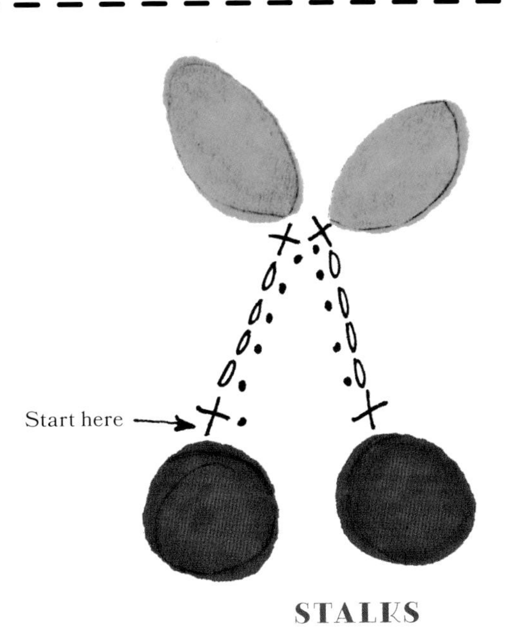

STALKS

STALKS

Row 1: With 2.5mm hook and B, work 1 dc into the top, gathered end of a cherry, 4 ch; with RS facing work 1 dc into 3-ch sp of each leaf, 4 ch, 1 dc into top of remaining cherry, turn.
Row 2: Sl st into each of the next 4 ch of the stalk just made, sl st into next 2 dc joining the leaves, sl st in next 4 ch of the first stalk.
Fasten off.

MAKING UP

Weave in all the yarn ends. Join the leaves about a third of the way up with a few stitches to keep them in place. Attach a brooch bar to the back of the double leaf. Sew through each hole on both sides, or around the bar if there are no holes.

WILD STRAWBERRY

This scrumptious pendant evokes memories of lazy days of summer all year round, with the succulent strawberry fruit highlighted by glistening embroidered seeds.

MATERIALS

- Crochet thread 20 in red (A), green (B) and black (C)
- Gold metallic embroidery thread
- 0.75mm (UK5:US12) crochet hook
- Toy stuffing
- Sewing needle

SIZE

Approximately ⅞in (2.25cm) at widest part
Approximately ⅞in (2.25cm) at longest part excluding loop

TENSION

52 sts and 50 rows to 4in (10cm) over double crochet using 0.75mm hook and A.
Use larger or smaller hook if necessary to obtain correct tension.

NOTE
1 ch at beg of the round does not count as a st throughout.

METHOD

The strawberry is worked in continuous rounds of double crochet and is similar to the heart patterns, with less shaping to the top. The leafy stalk is formed by working slip stitches into chain stitches, then attached to the top of the fruit, along with a short loop to hang from the necklace. Seeds are embroidered around the strawberry to decorate. The necklace is a length of chain stitches with a tiny crocheted button to fasten to a loop.

KEY

- chain (ch)
- slip stitch (sl st)
- double crochet (dc)
- dc2inc

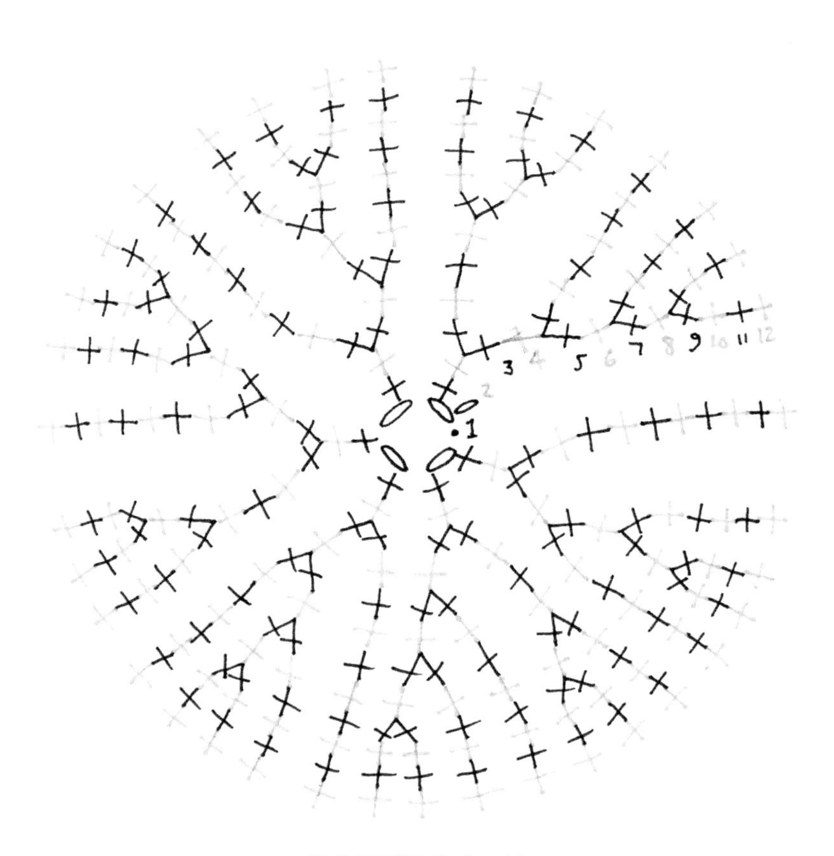

ROUNDS 1–12

STRAWBERRY

With 0.75mm hook and A, make 4 ch and join with a sl st to the first ch to form a ring.

Round 1: 1 ch, 6 dc into ring (6 sts).

Round 2: 1 dc in each st.

Round 3 (inc): (Dc2inc) 6 times (12 sts).

Round 4: 1 dc in each st.

Round 5 (inc): (Dc2inc, 1 dc) 6 times (18 sts).

Round 6: 1 dc in each st.

Round 7 (inc): (Dc2inc, 1 dc) 9 times (27 sts).

Round 8: 1 dc in each st.

Round 9 (inc): (Dc2inc, 2 dc) 9 times (36 sts).

Rounds 10–12: 1 dc in each st.

Shape top

Round 13: Work 1 dc in next 9 dc, skip next 18 sts, 1 dc in next 9 dc. Continue on these 18 sts.
Round 14: 1 dc in each st.
Fasten off, leaving a long tail of thread.
With RS facing, join A with a sl st to the first of the unworked 18 sts. Starting in the same dc as the sl st, work 2 rounds of 1 dc in each st to match first side. Fasten off, leaving a long tail of thread.

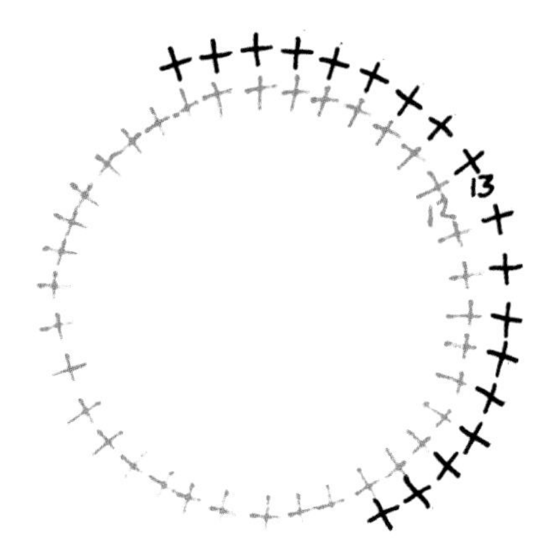

SHAPE TOP ROUND 13

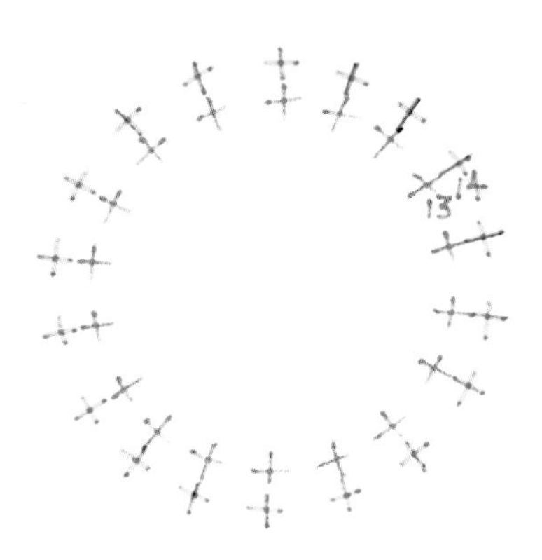

SHAPE TOP ROUND 14

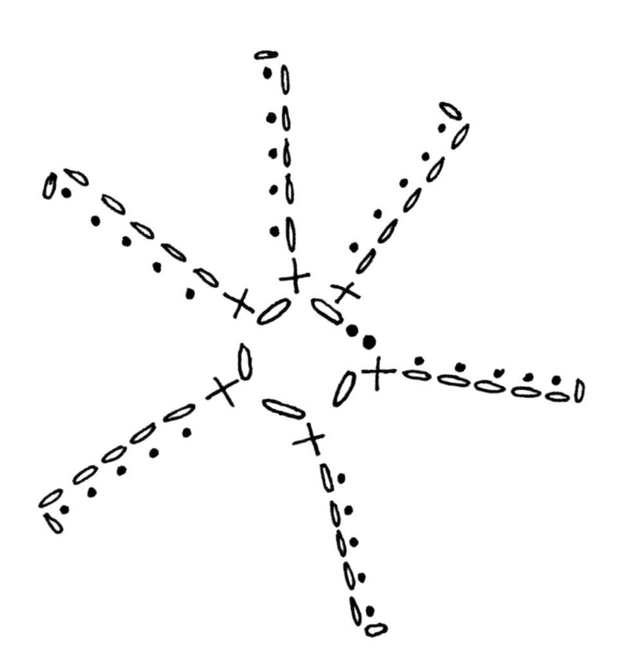
LEAFY STALK

LEAFY STALK

With 0.75mm hook and B, make 5 ch and join with a sl st to first ch to form a ring.
Next: (1 dc into ring, 6 ch, sl st in 2nd ch from hook, sl st in next 4 ch) 6 times, sl st into ring.
Fasten off, leaving a long tail of of thread.

NECKLACE

Button

Using 0.75mm hook and C, make 4 ch and join with sl st to first ch to form a ring.
Round 1: 1 ch, 6 dc into ring (6 sts).
Round 2 (inc): (Dc2inc) 6 times (12 sts).
Rounds 3–5: 1 dc in each st.
Fasten off, leaving a long tail of thread. Stuff the button firmly. Weave the tail of thread through the last round, pull tightly on the thread to close the opening and fasten off.

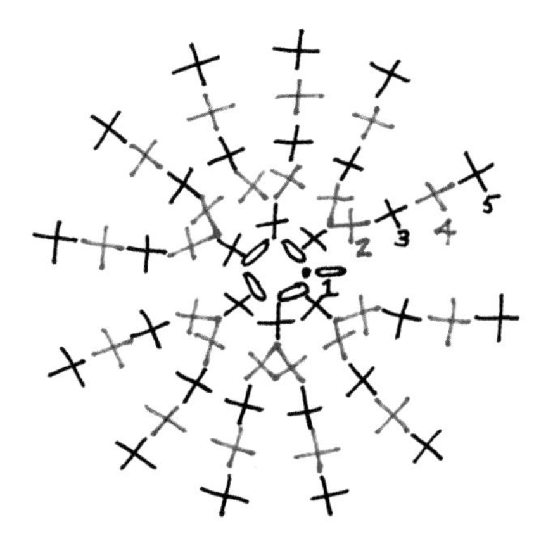

BUTTON

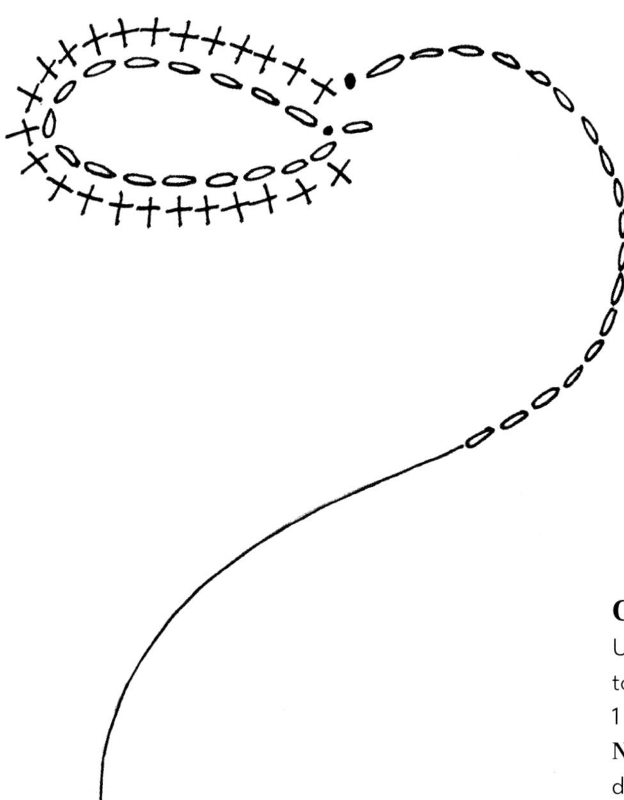

CHAIN AND LOOP

Chain and loop

Using 0.75mm hook and C, make 16 ch and join with sl st to first ch to form a ring.
1 ch, 24 dc into ring, sl st to first dc.
Next: Work a chain measuring 17in (43cm), or to your desired length, allowing an extra ⅝in (1.5cm) for attaching the strawberry.

MAKING UP

Stuff the strawberry firmly. Weave the tails of thread through the last round of stitches on each side of the top shaping, pull tightly on the thread to close the openings and fasten off. Using the tail of thread, sew the leafy stalk to the top of the fruit, working a few stitches into the lower part of the leaves to hold them in place. Weave in all the thread ends.

With 0.75mm hook and B, make 10 ch, sl st to first ch to form a loop. Fasten off and sew the loop to the centre of the leaf. Embroider seeds around the strawberry by working a number of bullion stitches (see below) in gold metallic thread. Attach the crocheted chain to the strawberry by folding it in half and threading the doubled chain through the loop at the top of the stalk. Take the button and loop at the ends of the chain and thread them back through the folded necklace. Pull on the ends to tighten the chain.

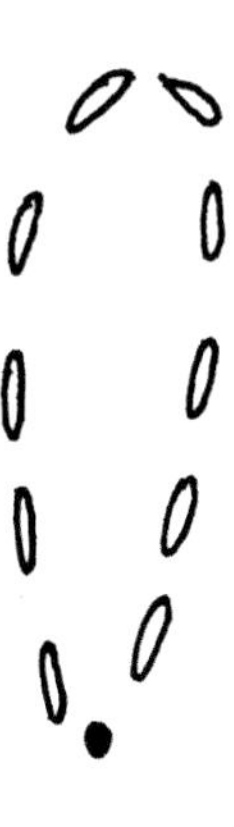

LOOP

BULLION STITCH

1. Using a needle with a narrow eye, bring the thread through to the front of the work at the position the bullion stitch is to be made. Work a backstitch to the required length of the finished bullion, bringing the needle out at the point where it first emerged. Wind the thread around the needle as many times as required to cover the space.

2. Hold the coiled thread down and carefully pull the needle through. Turn the coiled thread back towards the point where the needle was inserted and pass the needle back into the same place, pulling the thread through to the back of the work until the stitch lies flat.

OAK LEAF & ACORN

This sculptural piece of nature's bounty makes a subtle and elegant pendant, using cotton thread for the shiny nut and a lace-weight wool for the textured acorn hat.

MATERIALS

- Crochet thread 20 in rich dark brown (A) and green (B)
- Lace-weight wool or 2ply embroidery yarn in light brown (C)
- 0.75mm (UK5:US12) crochet hook
- Tiny amount of toy stuffing
- Sewing needle
- PVA glue

SIZE

Acorn is approximately ¾in (2cm) long
Oak leaf is approximately 1in (2.5cm) long

TENSION

52 sts and 50 rows to 4in (10cm) over double crochet using 0.75mm hook and A.
Use larger or smaller hook if necessary to obtain correct tension.

NOTE

1 ch at beg of the round does not count as a st throughout.

METHOD

The nut and acorn cups are finished separately and joined by a crocheted chain, which is slip stitched into to finish the stalk. Various stitches are used to shape the oak leaf. The empty cup and leaf are given a coating of PVA glue to stiffen the fabric and keep the shape. The necklace consists of a length of chain stitches, fastened by a crocheted loop and tiny nut. The acorn and leaf are separate pieces that are threaded on to the finished crocheted necklace.

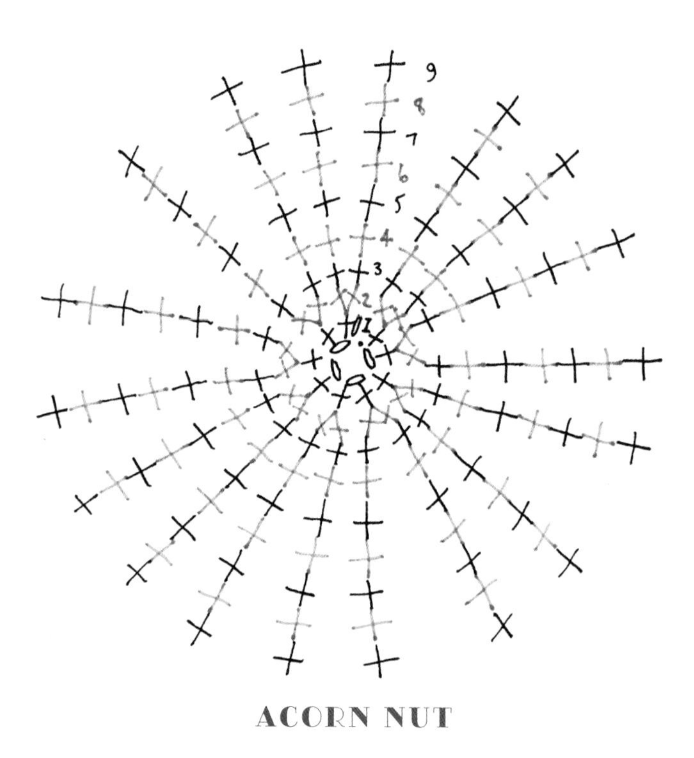

ACORN NUT

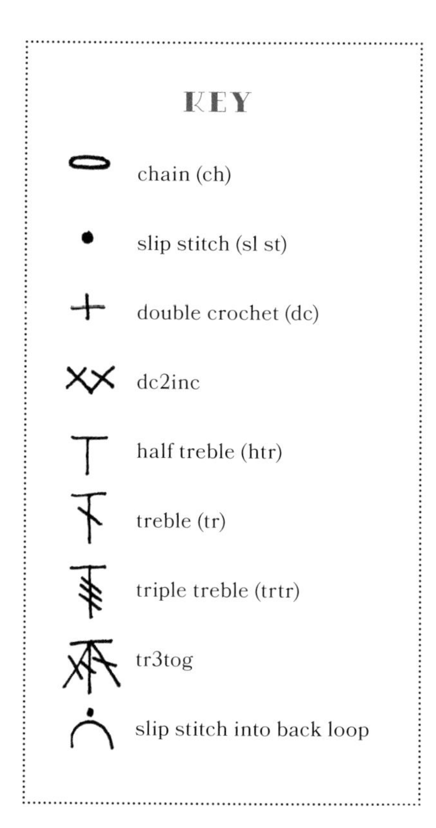

ACORN NUT

With 0.75mm hook and A, make 4 ch and join with a sl st to first ch to form a ring.

Round 1: 1 ch, 9 dc into ring (9 sts).

Round 2 (inc): (Dc2inc) 9 times (18 sts).

Rounds 3–9: 1 dc in each st.

Fasten off, leaving a long tail of thread. Stuff the nut and weave the tail of thread through the last round. Pull tightly on the thread to close the opening and fasten off. Weave in the ends.

ACORN HAT

With 0.75mm hook and C, make 5 ch and join with a sl st to first ch to form a ring.

Round 1: 1 ch, 10 dc into ring (10 sts).

Round 2 (inc): (Dc2inc) 10 times (20 sts).

Rounds 3–6: 1 dc in each st.

Sl st to next st. Fasten off, leaving a long tail of yarn to stitch the hat securely over the gathered end of the nut.

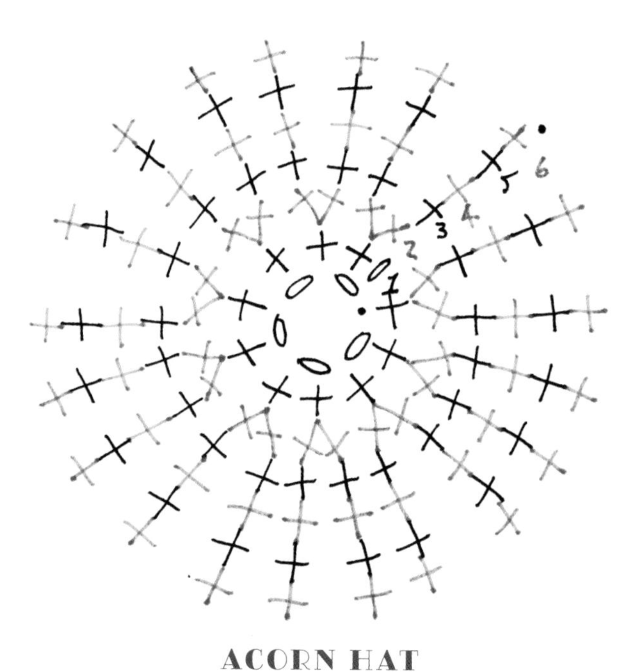

ACORN HAT

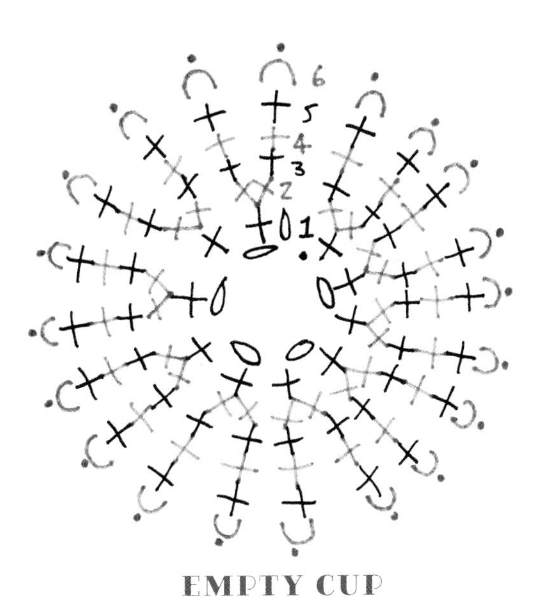

EMPTY CUP

EMPTY CUP

With 0.75mm hook and C, work as for the acorn hat to the end of round 2.
Rounds 3–5: 1 dc in each st.
Round 6: Sl st into back loops only of each dc.
Fasten off and weave in the yarn ends.

STALK

With 0.75mm hook and C, work 1 dc into the top of the acorn hat, 9 ch, 1 trtr into the top of the empty cup, 15 ch, sl st into the 10th ch from hook to form a loop, sl st into each of the ch, sl st into the first dc. Fasten off and weave in ends.

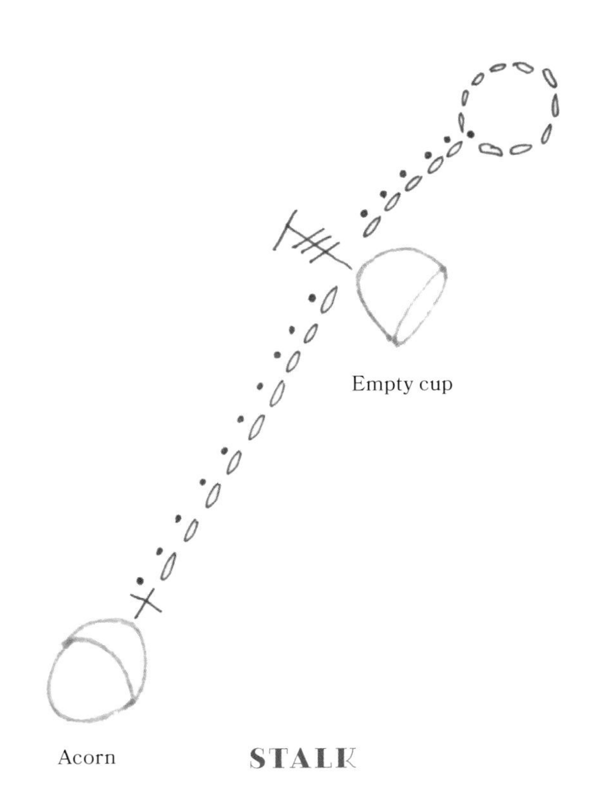

STALK

OAK LEAF

With 0.75mm hook and B, make 19 ch.
Sl st into 2nd ch from hook, sl st into next 17 ch.

Shape first side

Working down reverse side of ch, sl st into first st, (1 dc in next st, 1 htr in next st, 1 tr in next st, 4 ch, 1 dc into 2nd ch from hook, 1 htr in next ch, 1 tr in next ch, 1 dc in same st as the tr before the 4 ch shaping, skip 2 ch) 3 times.

Shape top

1 dc in next ch, 1 htr in next ch, 1 ch, tr3tog in end ch, 1 ch; working in back loops of sl sts, 1 htr in next st, 1 dc in next st.

Shape other side

(Skip 2 ch, 1 dc in back loop of next st, 4 ch, 1 dc in 2nd ch from hook, 1 htr in next ch, 1 tr in next ch, 1 tr in same st as the dc before the 4 ch shaping, 1 htr in back loop of next st, 1 dc in back loop of next st) 3 times, sl st to next st, 10 ch, sl st to first ch to form a loop. Fasten off and weave in ends.

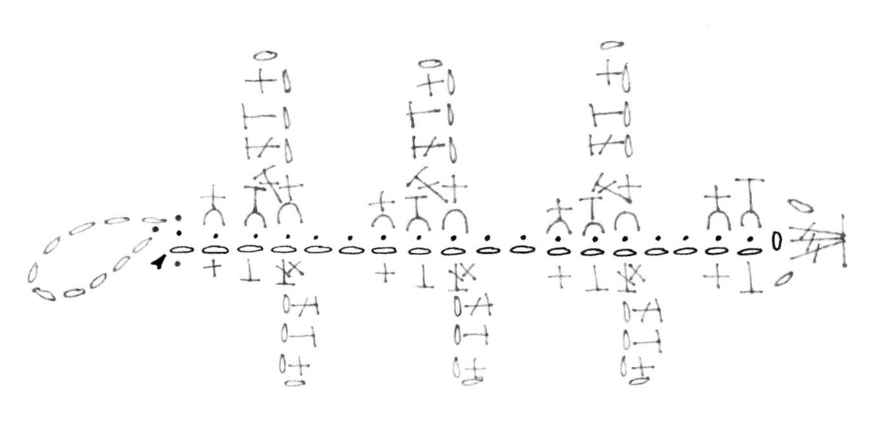

OAK LEAF

NECKLACE NUT BUTTON

NECKLACE NUT BUTTON

With 0.75mm hook and A, make 4 ch and join with a sl st to form a ring.

Round 1: 1 ch, 6 dc into ring (6 sts).

Round 2 (inc): (Dc2inc) 6 times (12 sts).

Rounds 3–6: 1 dc in each st.

Fasten off and weave the tail of thread through the last round. Stuff the nut and pull tightly on the thread to close the opening. Fasten off and weave in ends.

LOOP AND CHAIN

With 0.75mm hook and A, make 16 ch and join with a sl st to first ch to form a loop.

Next: 1 ch, 24 dc into loop, sl st to first dc. Make a chain measuring 17in (43cm), or to desired length, allowing an extra ⅝in (1.5cm) for attaching the acorn and leaf. Fasten off and sew nut button to end.

MAKING UP

Paint the inside of the empty cup and the back of the oak leaf with PVA glue, and leave to dry completely. Fold the chain in the middle to form a loop. Insert a crochet hook through the loop on the acorn stalk and the leaf, catch the folded necklace chain and draw it through. Pass the ends of the necklace through the looped chain. Pull tightly on ends to secure.

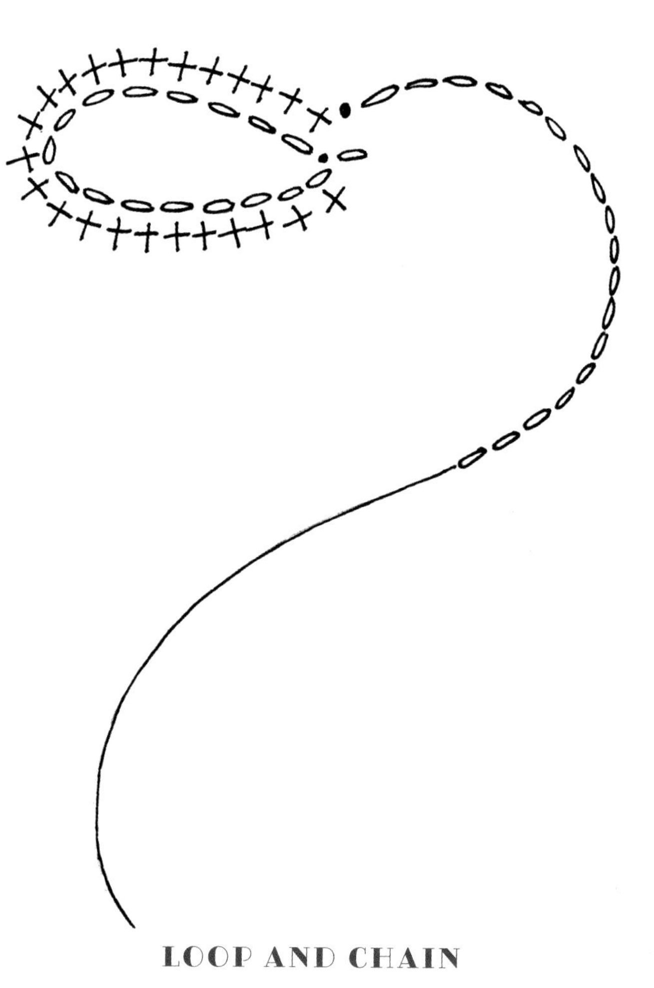

LOOP AND CHAIN

VARIATION: ACORN BUTTONHOLE

Make the acorn nut, hat and oak leaf as for the necklace.

LARGE BEAD

With 0.75mm hook and C, make 4 ch and join with a sl st to form a ring.
Round 1: 1 ch, 5 dc into ring (5 sts).
Round 2 (inc): (Dc2inc) 5 times (10 sts).
Rounds 3—9: 1 dc in each st.
Fasten off, leaving a long tail of yarn.
Stuff the beads firmly, using the end of the hook to push the stuffing down. Thread the tail of yarn through the last round of stitches, pull tightly on yarn to close the opening and fasten off. Weave in the yarn ends.

SMALL BEAD

With 0.75mm hook and C, make 4 ch and join with a sl st to form a ring.
Rounds 1—6: As for the large bead.
Finish as for the large bead.

STALK

With 0.75mm hook and C, work 1 dc into the top of the small bead, 9 ch, 1 tr into the top of the large bead, 17 ch, 1 dc into the 10-ch loop at the end of the leaf, 5 ch, 1 dc into the top of the acorn hat. Fasten off and weave in all the yarn ends.

VARIATION: LEAVES

Make the leaf using cotton 20 thread in autumnal shades, or two strands of gold metallic embroidery thread for an alternative finish.

HAIR ACCESSORIES, RINGS & BRACELETS

GIANT POPPY

With the use of textured yarns in striking colours and some shimmering sequins worked in to catch the light, this jolly oversized poppy hair adornment is guaranteed to turn heads!

MATERIALS

- Metallic yarn in black (A), 4ply yarn in a green-yellow shade (B) and pale pink or red (C)
- 2.5mm (UK12:US-) crochet hook
- 33 sequins
- Small amount of toy stuffing
- Length of hat elastic to fit head
- Blunt-ended yarn needle
- Sewing needle
- Sewing thread

SIZE

Approximately 6in (15cm) across petals

TENSION

26 sts and 26 rows to 10cm (4in) over double crochet using 2.5mm hook and A.
Use larger or smaller hook if necessary to obtain correct tension.

METHOD

This very large bloom uses the long treble and double treble stitches to form the petals. The repetitive pattern around each petal makes this a great project with which to practise the more complicated stitches. The sequinned centre is worked first and attached to the petals to finish the poppy. A brooch bar can be sewn to the back of the flower to wear as a corsage.

NOTES

1 ch at beg of the round does not count as a st throughout.

3 ch at beg of the round counts as a st throughout.

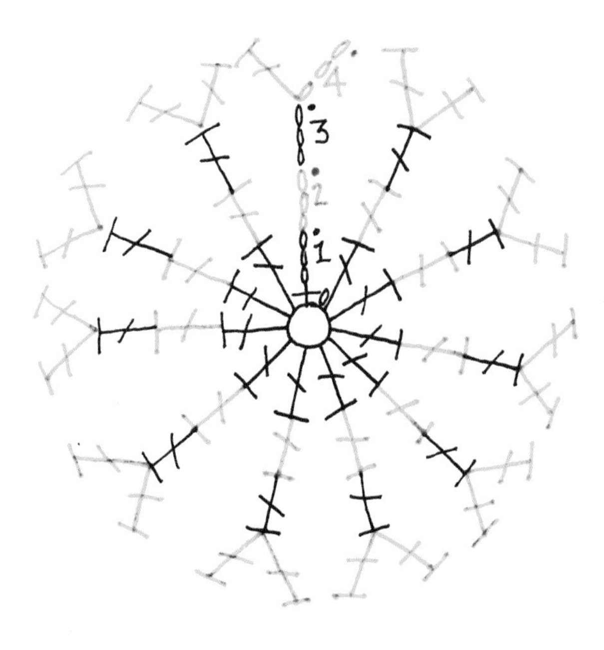

POPPY CENTRE ROUNDS 1–4

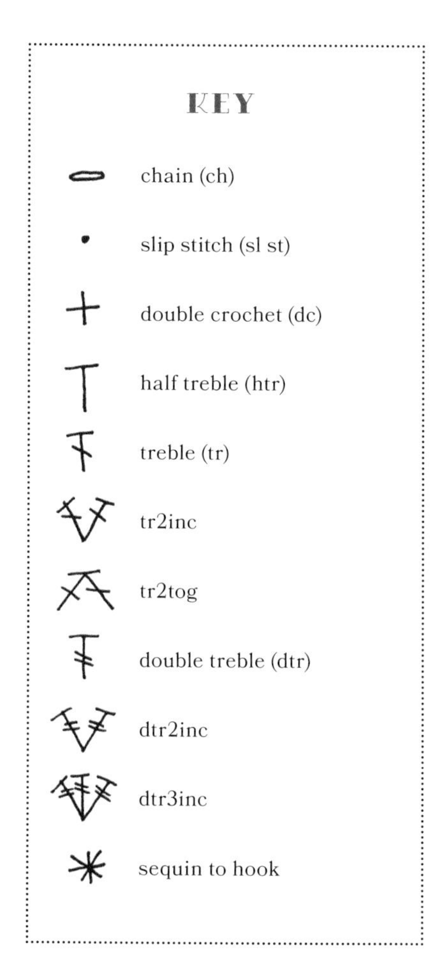

POPPY CENTRE

Thread 33 sequins on to yarn A.

With 2.5mm hook and A, make a magic loop.

Round 1 (RS): 1 ch, 1 dc into loop, 3 ch, 10 tr into loop, sl st to 3rd of 3 ch with B. Pull tightly on short end of yarn to close loop (11 sts).

Carry yarn A on WS of work.

Rounds 2–3: 3 ch, 1 tr in each tr, sl st to 3rd of 3 ch with A.

Continue with A.

Round 4 (inc): 3 ch, 1 tr in same st as sl st, (tr2inc) 10 times, sl st to 3rd of 3 ch, turn to WS (22 sts).

Continue on WS of work. The sequins will appear on the RS.

Rounds 5–7 (WS): 3 ch, (bring sequin to hook, 1 ch, 1 tr in next 2 tr) 10 times, sequin to hook, 1 ch, 1 tr in next tr, sl st to 3rd of 3 ch.

Round 8: 3 ch, 1 tr in each tr, sl st in 3rd of 3 ch.

Round 9 (dec): 3 ch, 1 tr in next tr, (tr2tog) 10 times, sl st to 3rd of 3 ch (12 sts).

Rounds 10–11: 3 ch, 1 tr in each tr, sl st to 3rd of 3 ch.

Fasten off, leaving a long tail of both yarns.

Stuff the yellow part of the centre. Thread the tail of yarn B around the lower edges of the centre piece, between rounds 3 and 4, pull tightly on the yarn to gather the stitches and fasten off. Thread the tail of yarn A through the last round of stitches, pull tightly on yarn to close the opening and fasten off. Push the yellow centre inside the sequinned black section, which will form a collar around the stuffed centre. Stitch in place by pushing the needle several times right through the work, from the base of the sequinned section to the metallic tip of the yellow centre.

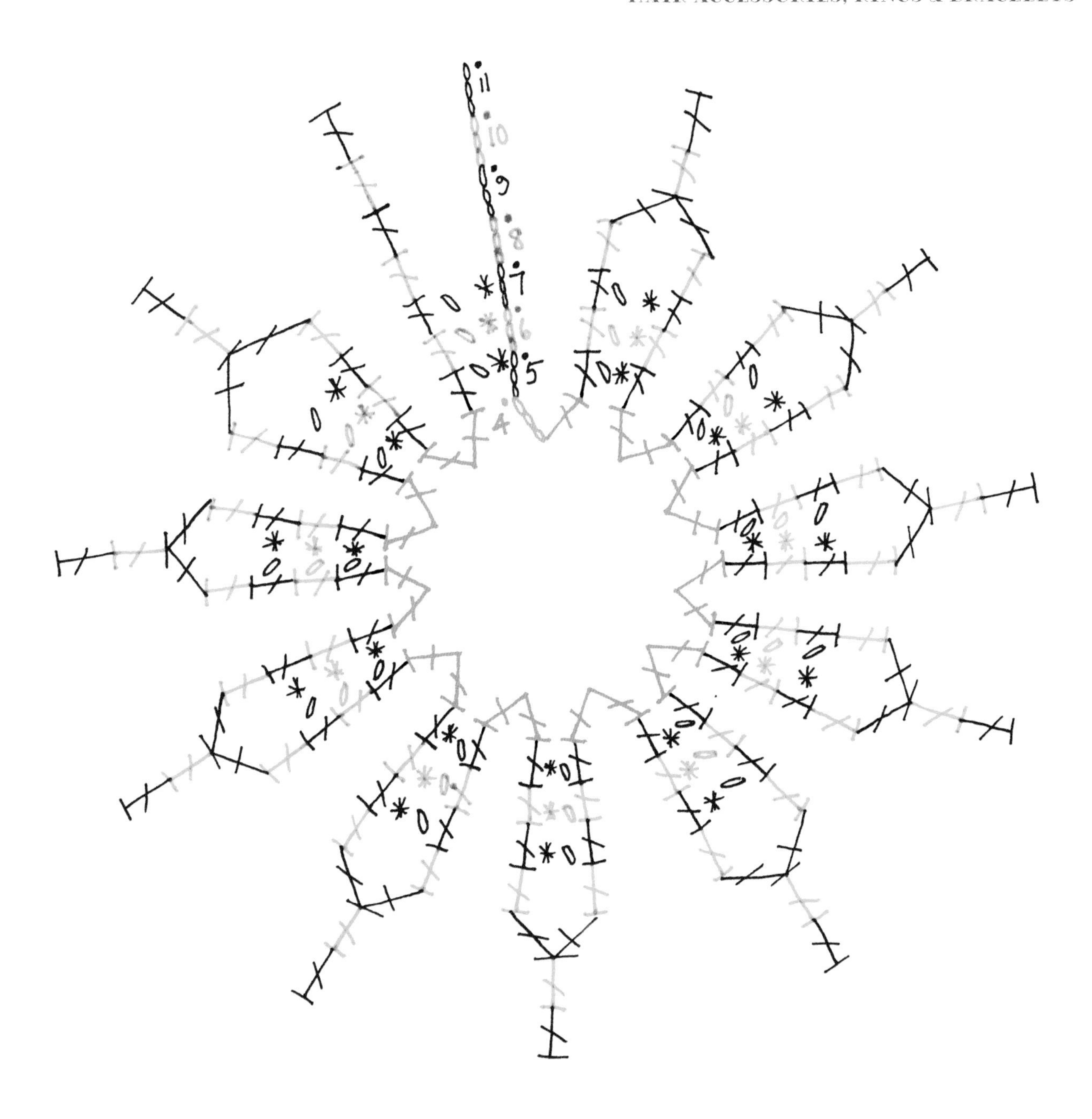

ROUNDS 5–11

PETALS

With 2.5mm hook and A, make 6 ch and join with a sl st to first ch to form a ring.

Round 1 (RS): 3 ch, 2 tr into ring, (9 ch, 3 tr) 3 times, 9 ch, sl st to 3rd of 3 ch (12 tr and 4 9-ch sps).

Round 2: *Skip next tr, 1 dc in next tr, skip next tr, (4 dc, 2 htr, 2 tr, 5 dtr, 2 tr, 2 htr, 4 dc) into next 9-ch sp*; rep from * to * 3 more times, sl st to first dc, sl st up next 4 dc of first petal. Join C in last sl st.

Continue with C.

Round 3 (inc): *1 htr in next 2 htr, 1 tr in next tr, (dtr3inc, dtr2inc) 3 times, dtr3inc, 1 tr in next tr, 1 htr in next 2 htr, skip next 4 dc down side of petal, skip 1 dc in between petals, skip 4 dc up side of next petal*; rep from * to * 3 more times (96 sts).

Round 4 (inc): *1 htr in next 2 htr, 1 tr in next tr, dtr2inc in next 18 sts, 1 tr in next tr, 1 htr in next 2 htr*; rep from * to * 3 more times, sl st to next htr, turn to WS (168 sts).

Round 5 (WS) (inc): *Skip next htr, 1 htr in next htr, 1 tr in next tr, dtr2inc in next 36 sts, 1 tr in next tr, 1 htr in next htr, skip next htr*; rep from * to * 3 more times, sl st in next st (304 sts).

Fasten off.

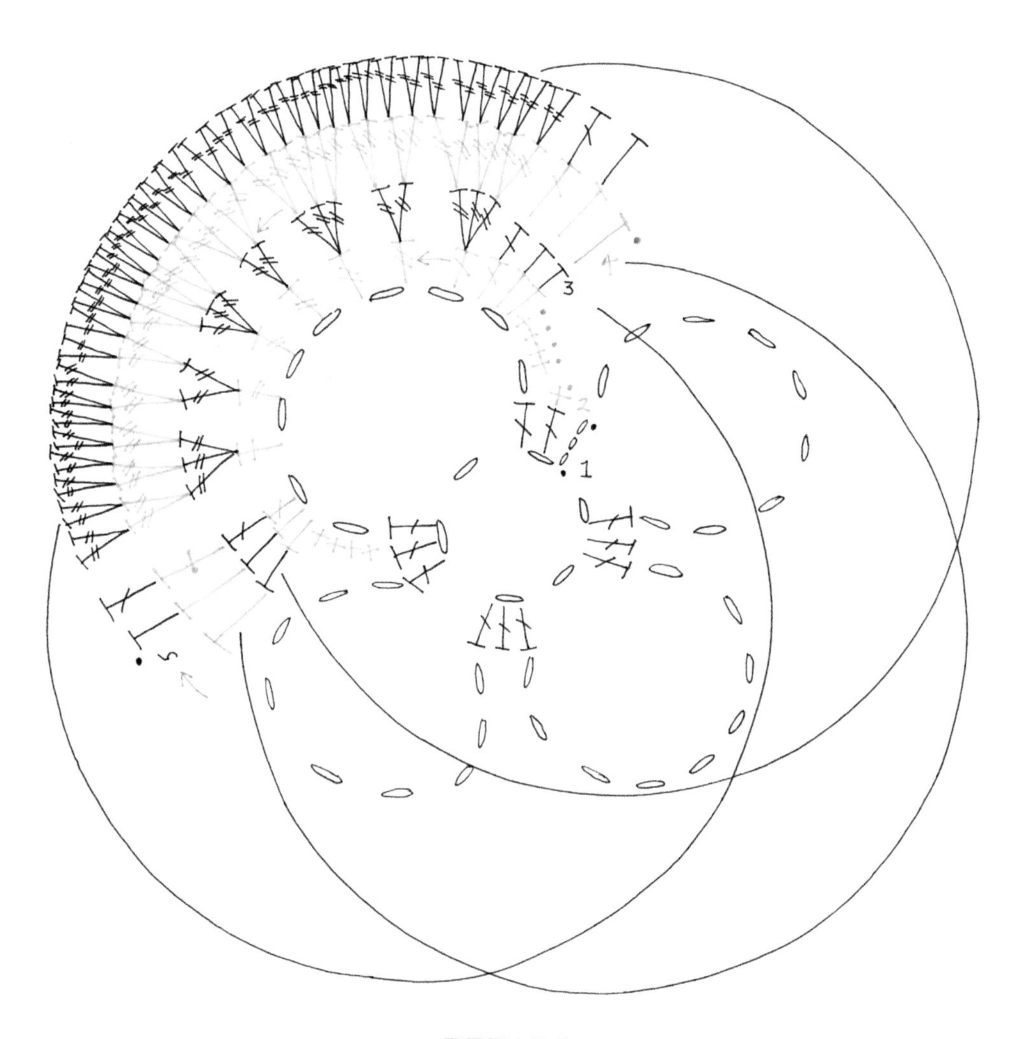

PETALS

MAKING UP

Attach the poppy centre to the middle of the petals on the RS. Weave in all the yarn ends. Sew the length of hat elastic to the base of the poppy.

DAFFODIL

Bring spring to your wardrobe with this bright headband. By replacing the band with a hairclip or brooch bar, this colourful accessory can be worn in a variety of ways.

MATERIALS

- Oddments of DK yarn in white (A), orange (B), green (C) and black (D)
- Oddment of black metallic yarn (E)
- 3mm (UK11:USC2/D3) crochet hook
- Blunt-ended yarn needle

SIZE

Approximately 4⅜in (11cm) across leafy base

TENSION

22 sts and 24 rows to 4in (10cm) over double crochet using 3mm hook and A.
Use larger or smaller hook if necessary to obtain correct tension.

NOTES

1 ch at beg of the row/round does not count as a st throughout.

3 ch at beg of the row/round counts as first treble throughout.

METHOD

The petals, trumpet, bead and the headband itself are all crocheted separately and stitched together to make up the finished piece. Various stitches are used to shape the petals. The band is worked in rows using treble stitches to create an open-weave fabric.

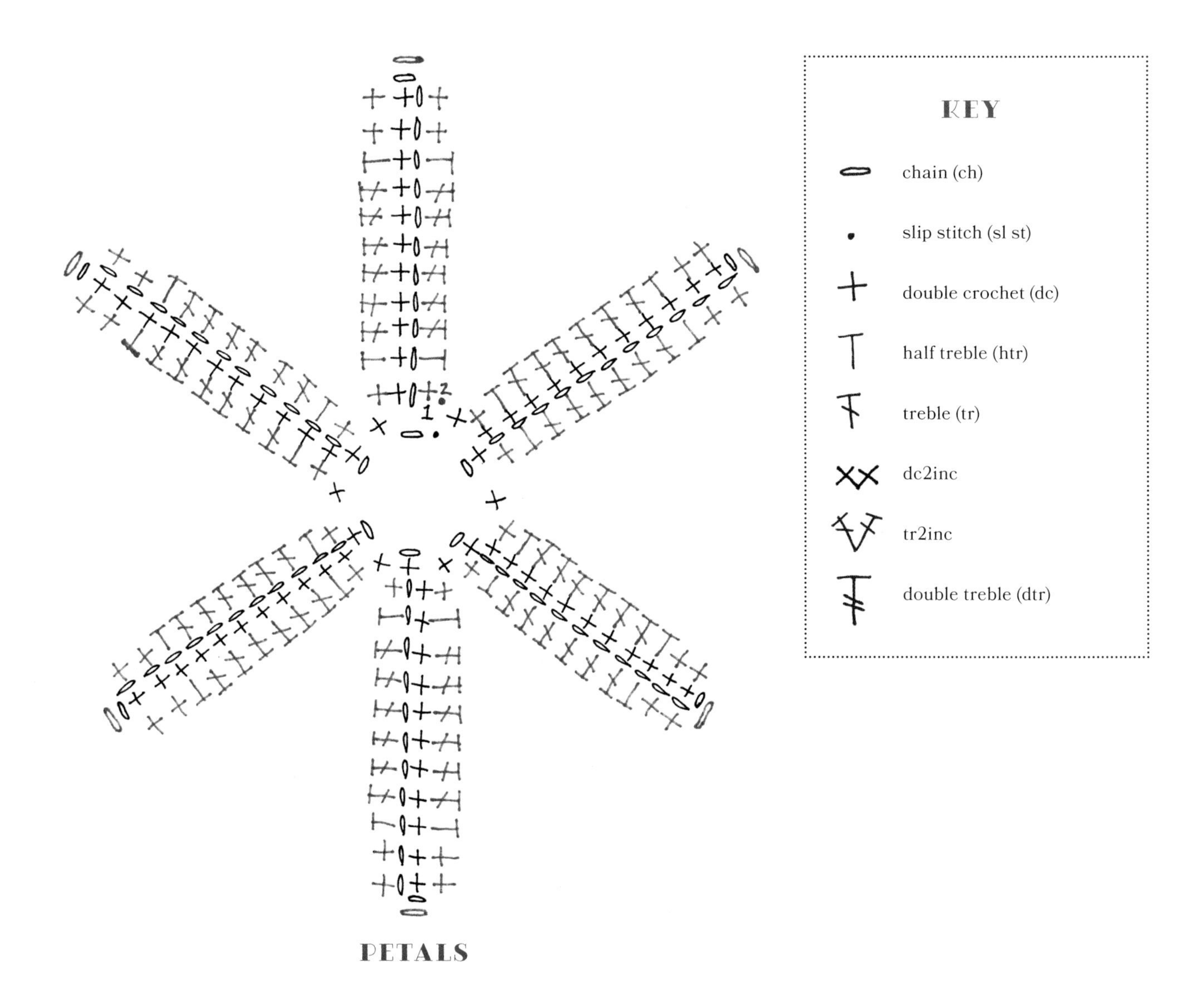

PETALS

PETALS

With 3mm hook and A, make 6 ch and join with a sl st to first ch to form a ring.

Round 1: (12 ch, 1 dc into 2nd ch from hook, 1 dc in next 10 ch, 2 dc into ring) 5 times, 12 ch, 1 dc into 2nd ch from hook, 1 dc in next 10 ch, 1 dc into ring (6 spokes).

Round 2: (Working into the other side of each ch, 1 dc into first ch, 1 htr in next ch, 1 tr in next 6 ch, 1 htr in next ch, 1 dc in next 2 ch, 1 ch, 1 dc in next 2 dc down other side of petal, 1 htr in next dc, 1 tr in next 6 dc, 1 htr in next dc, 1 dc in next dc) 6 times, sl st to first dc (6 petals). Fasten off.

TRUMPET

With 3mm hook and B, leaving a long length of yarn at the beginning, make 4 ch and join with a sl st to first ch to form a ring.

Round 1: 1 ch, 7 dc into ring (7 sts).

Round 2 (inc): (Dc2inc) 7 times (14 sts).

Rounds 3–6: 1 dc in each st.

Round 7 (inc): 3 ch, 1 tr in same st, (tr2inc) 13 times, sl st to 3rd of 3 ch (28 sts).

Fasten off.

TRUMPET

LEAFY BASE

LEAFY BASE

With 3mm hook and C, make 5 ch and join with a sl st to first ch to form a ring.

Round 1: 3 ch, 11 tr into ring, sl st to 3rd of 3 ch (12 sts).

Round 2 (inc): 3 ch, 1 tr in same st, (tr2inc) 11 times, sl st to 3rd of 3 ch (24 sts).

Round 3: 9 ch, skip first tr, (1 dc in next 3 tr, 8 ch, skip next tr) 5 times, 1 dc in next 2 tr (6 loops).

Round 4: (3 dc, 1 htr, 2 tr, 4 dtr, 2 tr, 1 htr, 3 dc) into each loop, sl st to first dc (96 sts).

Fasten off.

BEAD

With 3mm hook and E, make 5 ch and join with a sl st to form a ring.
Next: 3 ch, work 17 tr into ring, sl st to 3rd of 3 ch. Fasten off, leaving a long tail of yarn. Thread the tail through the top of the stitches. Pull tightly on the yarn to close the opening, forming a large bead. Fasten off.

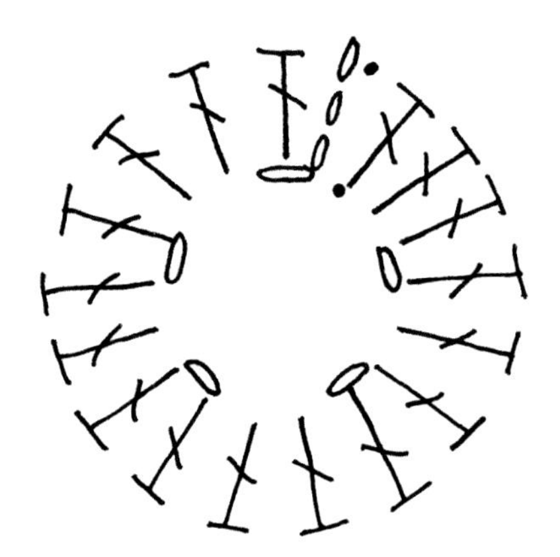

BEAD

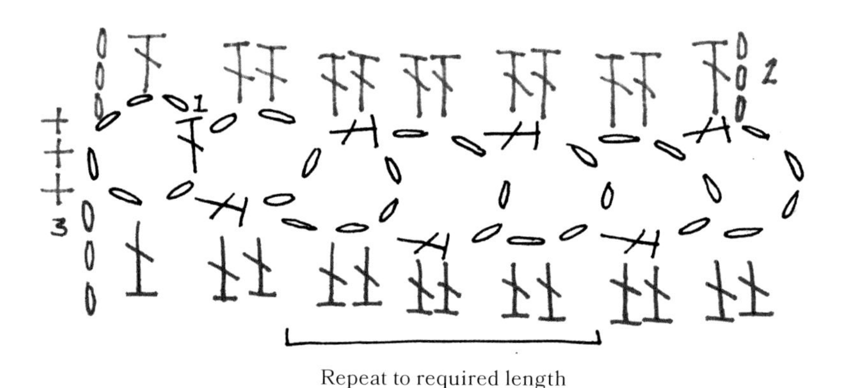

HEADBAND

HEADBAND

With 3mm hook and D, make 6 ch.
Row 1: 1 tr in first ch to join and make first space, 4 ch, turn, 1 tr into 6-ch sp, *4 ch, turn, 1 tr into 4-ch sp; rep from * to make the required length to fit around head without stretching, as the finished piece will be tighter.
Row 2: 3 ch, 1 tr in first 4-ch sp, 2 tr in all but last 6-ch sp, 1 tr in last 6-ch sp, 3 ch, 3 dc in last 6-ch sp.
Row 3: Rotate the piece and, working into the opposite side of each space, 3 ch, 1 tr in first sp, 2 tr in each 4-ch sp to end. Fasten off, leaving a long tail of yarn.

MAKING UP

Stitch the bead to the inside of the trumpet. Sew the trumpet to the centre of the daffodil petals, using the length of yarn left at the beginning. Place the finished flower on the RS of the leafy base, positioning the petals in between the leaves. Sew neatly in place. Join the short ends of the crocheted band and attach the daffodil. Weave in all the yarn ends.

CHARM BRACELET

The ancient tradition of adorning a simple chain with pendants is the inspiration for this project. Here, colourful trinkets decorate a pretty crocheted bracelet with an adjustable fastening.

MATERIALS

- Oddments of 4ply yarn in 5 colours (A, B, C, D and E), oddment of 4ply yarn in contrast shade for heart (F)
- Metallic yarn for chain and leaves (G)
- 2.5mm (UK12:US-) crochet hook
- Sewing thread
- 9 x sequins
- 1 x ⅛in (4mm) pearl bead
- 10 x seed beads
- 1 x faceted bead
- 1 x head pin
- Toy stuffing
- Blunt-ended yarn needle
- Sewing needle
- Round-nose pliers
- Cutting pliers
- A keyring for each charm (variations only)

SIZE

Approximate length of bracelet: 8in (20cm)

NOTE

1 ch at beg of the row/round does not count as a st throughout.

TENSION

26 sts and 26 rows to 10cm (4in) over double crochet using 2.5mm hook and A.
Use larger or smaller hook if necessary to obtain correct tension.

METHOD

Each charm and leaf is made individually, using a variety of stitches and simple increasing and decreasing to form the shaping. The ribbed pattern of the cupcake case is made by crocheting into the horizontal loop below that of the normal loop of the stitch to be worked. Beads and sequins decorate the charms which, along with the leaves, are attached to the chain as it is crocheted.

KEY

Symbol	Meaning	Symbol	Meaning
	chain (ch)		half treble (htr)
	slip stitch (sl st)		htr2inc
	double crochet (dc)		treble (tr)
	dc2inc		double crochet into horizontal loop below loop of stitch on previous row
	slip stitch together back loops on each side to join		dc into back loop
	slip stitch into back loop only		

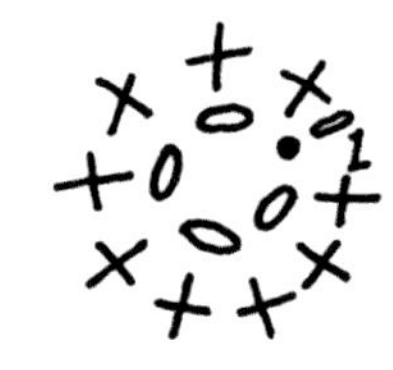

BUTTONHOLE

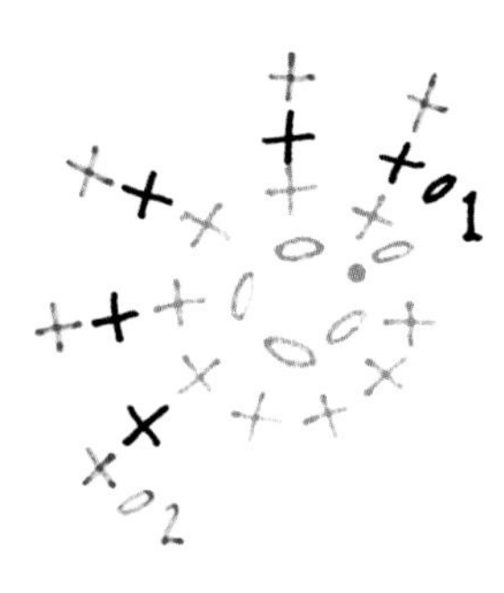

FLAP ROWS 1–2

BAG

Buttonhole

With 2.5mm hook and A, make 4 ch, join with a sl st to first ch to form a ring.

Round 1: 1 ch, 9 dc into ring (9 sts).

Flap

Row 1 (RS): 1 dc in next 5 dc, turn, leaving the last 4 sts unworked.

Row 2 (WS): 1 ch, 1 dc in next 5 dc, turn.

Body

The following is worked in continuous rounds.

Round 1 (RS): 6 ch, 1 dc in 2nd ch from hook, 1 dc in next 4 ch, 1 dc in next 5 dc, sl st to first dc to join.

Round 2 (RS): 1 dc in same st as sl st, 1 dc in next 9 dc (10 sts).

Round 3 (inc): Dc2inc, 1 dc in next 3 dc, (dc2inc) twice, 1 dc in next 3 dc, dc2inc (14 sts).

Round 4: 1 dc in each st.

Round 5 (inc): Dc2inc, 1 dc in next 5 dc, (dc2inc) twice, 1 dc in next 5 dc, dc2inc (18 sts).

Round 6: 1 dc in each st.

Next: Fold work and sl st tog the back loops of 9 sts on each side of bag to join. Fasten off.

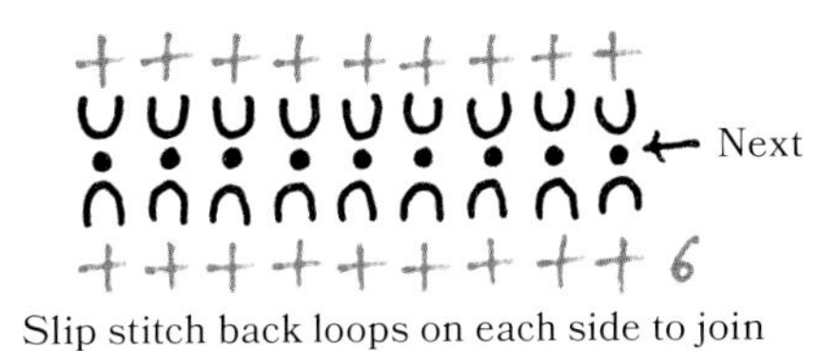

BAG BODY

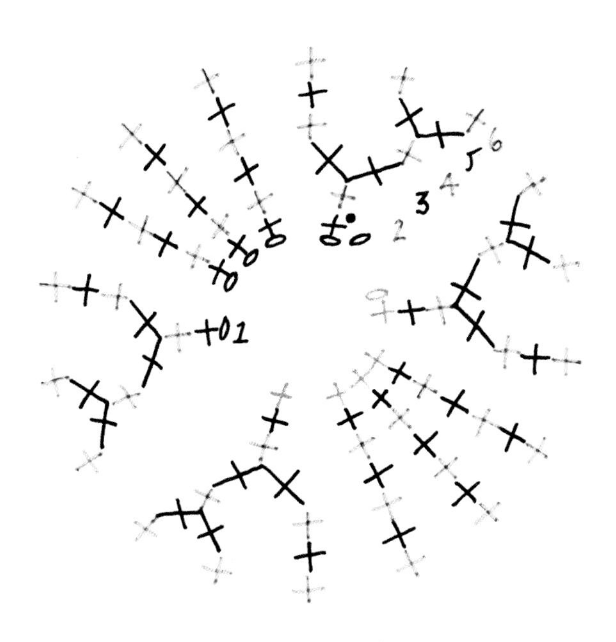

BODY ROUNDS 1–6

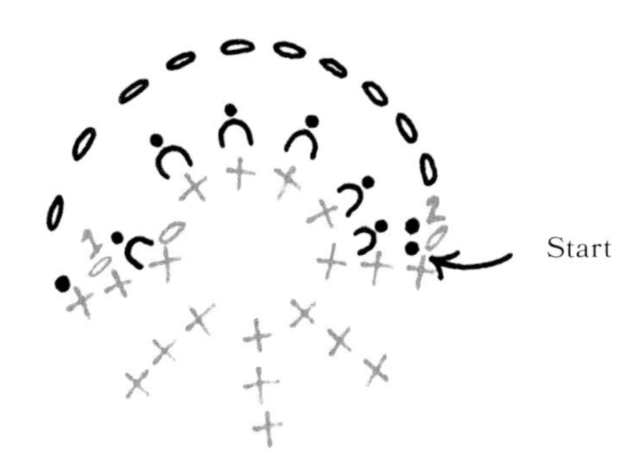

DECORATIVE EDGING AND HANDLE

Decorative edging and handle

With RS of back of bag facing, join B with a sl st to the edge of row 2 of the bag flap, sl st into the back loops of the next 6 stitches around the bag flap, sl st into opposite side of row 2 of flap, make 10 ch and sl st in the same place on first side to form the bag handle. Fasten off and weave in ends.

Sequin fringe

Thread 9 sequins onto sewing thread doubled and, with 2.5mm hook and back of bag facing, join thread with a sl st to the back loop of the first sl st at the joined, lower edge, sequin to hook, 1 ch, 1 dc into back loop of first st, (sequin to hook, 1 ch, 1 dc into back loop of next st) 8 times. These stitches will be loose due to the fine thread, allowing the sequins to move freely and catch the light. Fasten off and weave in ends. Sew a 4mm pearl bead to the straight edge, under the flap, for the button. Button up the bag.

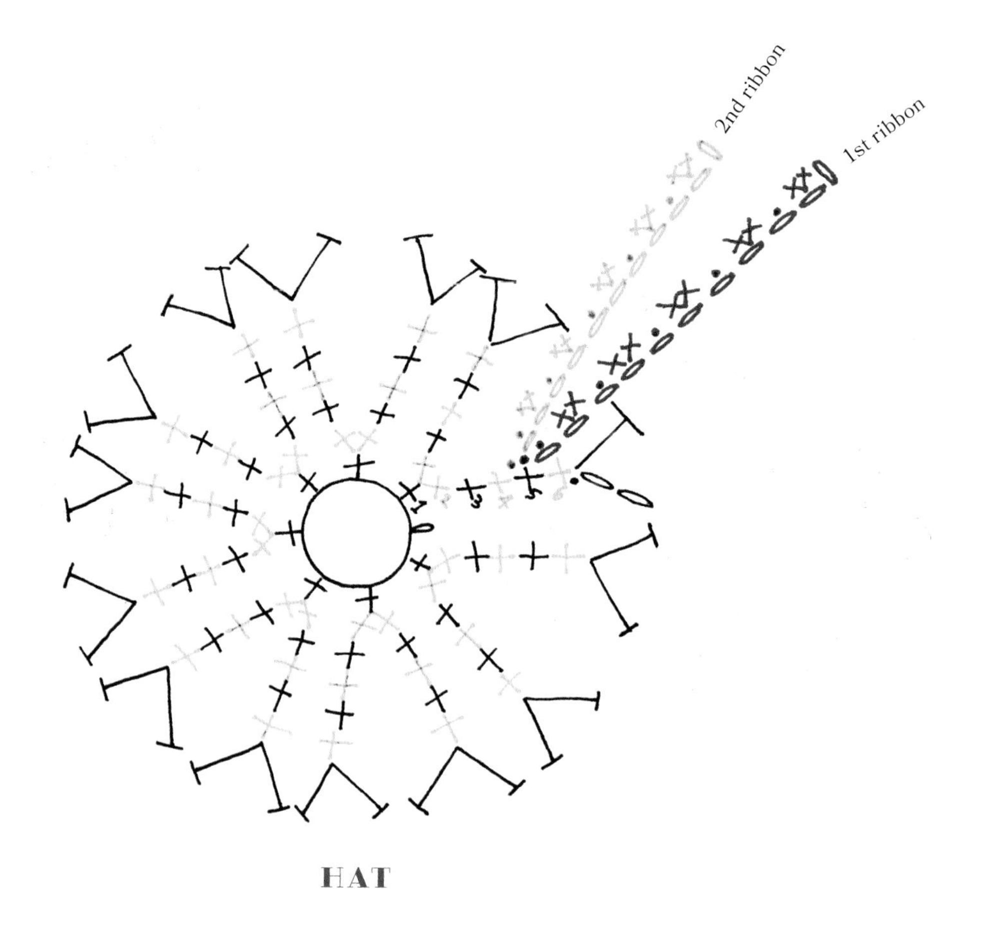

HAT

HAT

Crown

Using C and 2.5mm hook, make a magic loop.

Round 1: 1 ch, 7 dc into loop (7 sts).

Round 2 (inc): (Dc2inc) 7 times (14 sts). Pull on short end of yarn to close ring.

Rounds 3–4: 1 dc in each st. Join A in last dc of last round.

Rounds 5–6: 1 dc in each st with A. Do not fasten off.

Brim

Round 7: With C, sl st to next dc, 2 ch, 1 htr in same dc as sl st, (htr2inc) 13 times, sl st to 2nd of 2 ch, ensuring yarn A is at the front of the work (28 sts). Fasten off C and leave A attached.

Curly ribbons

With RS of hat facing, insert hook at the start of round 5 in A around the post of the stitch, catch the length of yarn still attached and draw back through, *11 ch, 2 dc in 2nd ch from hook, (sl st in next ch, 2 dc in next ch) 4 times, sl st in next ch, sl st into hat*. Rep from * to *. Fasten off and weave in ends. Twist each ribbon to curl.

SHOE

Sole

With D and 2.5mm hook, *make 4 ch and join with a sl st to first ch to form ring.

Round 1: 1 ch, 9 dc into ring (9 sts).

Round 2: 7 ch, 1 dc into 2nd ch from hook, 1 dc into next 5 ch, 1 dc into next 9 dc, 1 dc down opposite side of next 6 ch (21 sts). Fasten off and weave in ends.*

Insole

Using C and 2.5mm hook, rep from * to *.

Upper

Round 3: Place the sole and insole with WS together, matching the sts.

With 2.5mm hook and the sole facing, skip the first 6 sts and join B with a sl st to the next st on both pieces, 1 dc in same st as sl st, 1 dc in next 20 dc of both pieces at the same time to join (21 sts).

Round 4: 1 dc in each st.

Round 5: (Skip 1 dc, 1 dc in next dc) 4 times, sl st to next st. Fasten off and weave in loose ends.

Edging and laces

Round 6: Skip the first 2 dc at front of shoe and insert 2.5mm hook on the inside of the shoe into the next dc, catch yarn E and draw back through, leaving a long tail on the RS to tie into a bow at the end. With RS facing, starting in the same dc, sl st into back loops only of next 8 sts, finishing at the centre back of the heel, 5 ch, sl st into same st as last sl st to form loop, sl st into next 8 dc, finishing at the front of shoe. Fasten off, leaving a long tail of yarn for the bow. Tie the tails of yarn into a bow with a double knot so it won't come undone. Trim ends. Paint a tiny amount of PVA glue on ends to prevent them fraying.

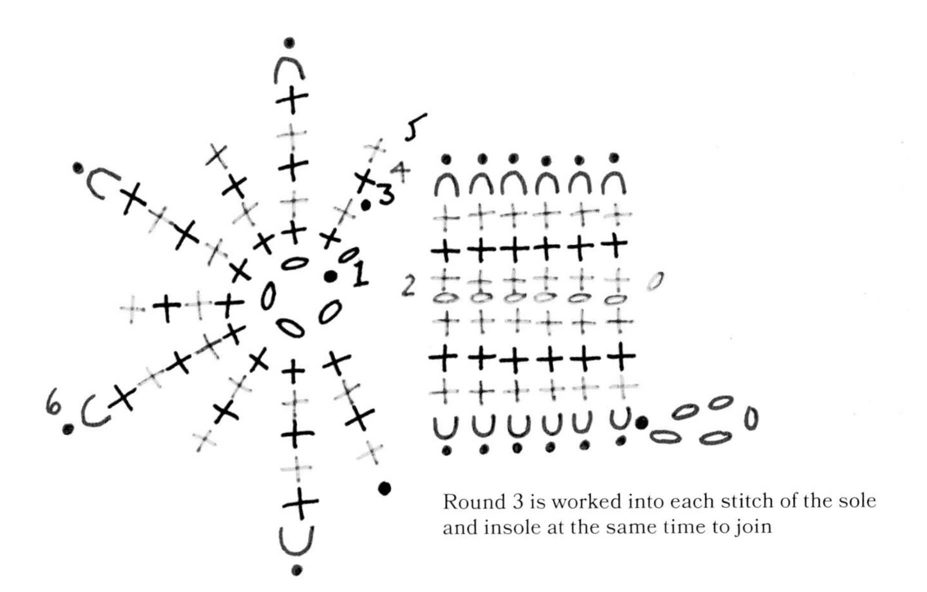

Round 3 is worked into each stitch of the sole and insole at the same time to join

SHOE

HEART

With F and 2.5mm hook, make a magic loop.

Round 1: 1 ch, 5 dc into loop (5 sts).

Round 2: 1 dc in each st, pull tightly on short end of yarn to close loop.

Round 3 (inc): (Dc2inc) 5 times (10 sts).

Round 4: 1 dc in each st.

Round 5 (inc): (Dc2inc) 10 times (20 sts).

Round 6: 1 dc in each st.

Shape top

Round 7: 1 dc in next 5 dc, skip next 10 sts, 1 dc in next 5 dc.

Continue on these 10 sts.

Round 8: 1 dc in each st.

Fasten off, leaving a long tail of yarn.

With RS facing, join F with a sl st to the first of the unworked 10 sts. Starting in the same dc as the sl st, work 2 rounds of 1 dc in each st to match first side.

Fasten off, leaving a long tail of yarn.

Stuff the heart. Thread the tail of yarn through the stitches of the last round, pull tightly on the yarn to close the opening and fasten off. Repeat to finish the other side of the top shaping. Weave in all the ends.

Thread a bead onto a head pin and poke through the tip of the heart. Use round-nose pliers to curl the end of the wire around the pin and trim with cutting pliers.

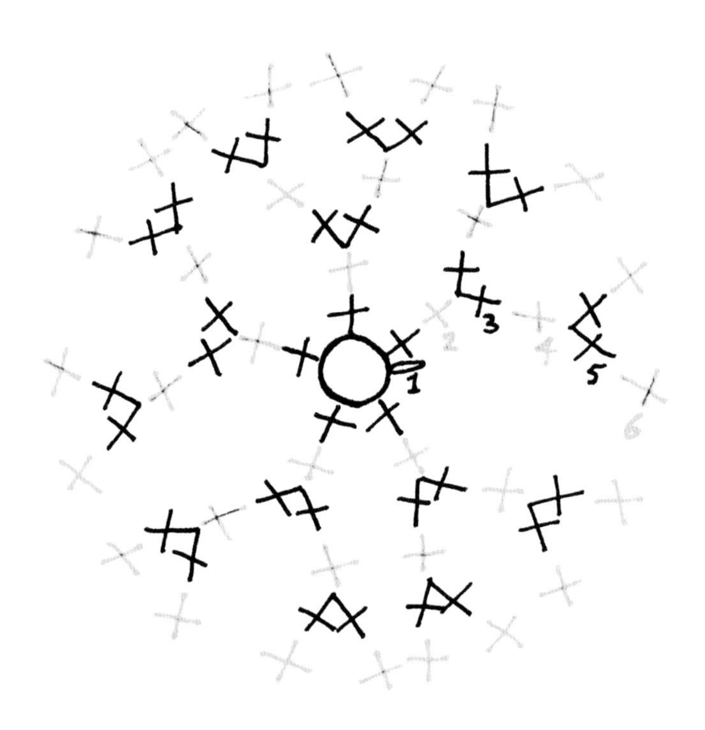

HEART ROUNDS 1–6

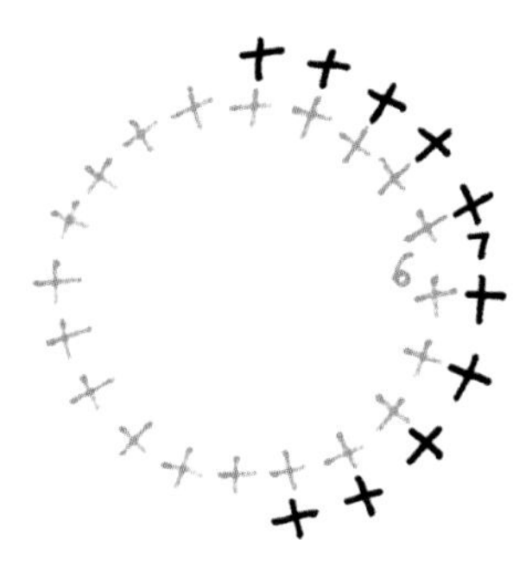

HEART SHAPE TOP ROUND 7

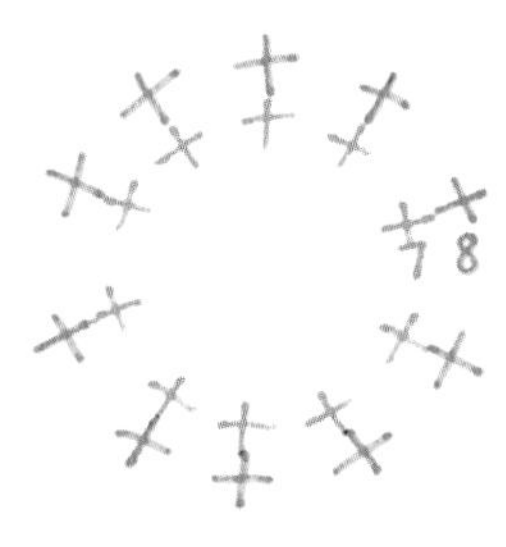

HEART SHAPE TOP ROUND 8

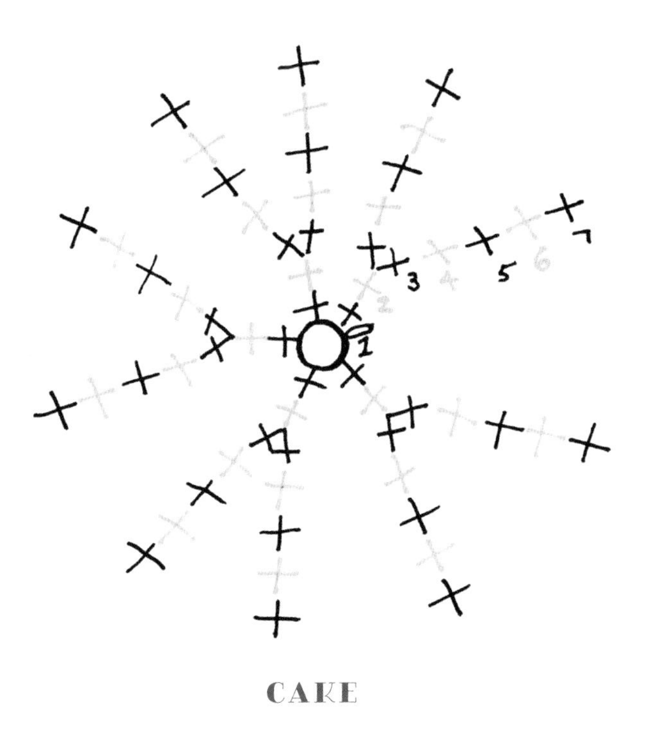

CAKE

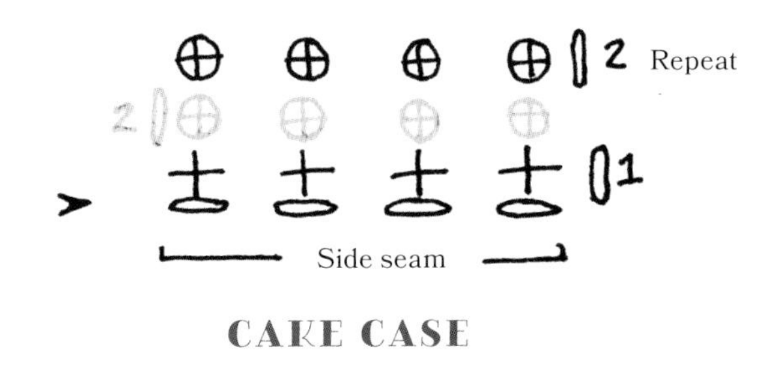

CAKE CASE

CUPCAKE

Cake

With E and 2.5mm hook, make a magic loop.
Round 1: 1 ch, 5 dc into loop (5 sts).
Round 2: 1 dc into each st. Pull tightly on short end of yarn to close ring.
Round 3 (inc): (Dc2inc) 5 times (10 sts).
Rounds 4–7: 1 dc in each st.
Fasten off and thread tail of yarn through rem sts. Stuff the cake. Pull tightly on end of yarn to close the opening and fasten off. Weave in ends.

Cake case

For a simple cake case pattern, see the variation on page 127.
With D and 2.5mm hook, make 5 ch that will form the side seam, rather than the lower edge.

CAKE CASE

Row 1: 1 dc into 2nd ch from hook, 1 dc in next 3 ch, turn (4 sts).
Row 2: 1 ch, 1 dc in each of the horizontal loops that lay below the loop of the dc on previous row, turn (see photograph). Rep row 2 until work fits snugly around the cake.
Fasten off, leaving a long tail of yarn.

Cake base

With D and 2.5mm hook, make 4 ch, join with sl st to first ch to form a ring.

Round 1: 1 ch (does not count as st), 5 dc into ring (5 sts).

Round 2: Dc2inc (5 times), sl st to next st (10 sts).

Fasten off. Use the tail of yarn to join the short edges of the cake case and stitch around cake. Sew the base to the case. Sew a scattering of seed beads over the top for decoration.

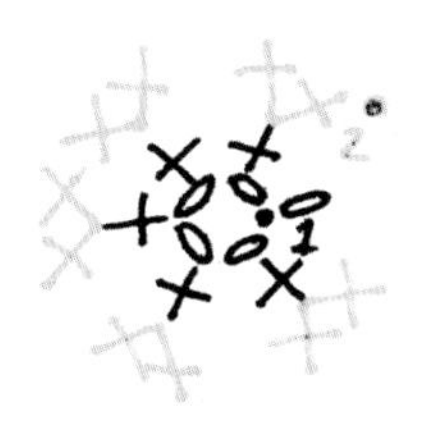

CAKE BASE

LEAVES (MAKE 6)

With G and 2.5mm hook, make 8 ch.

Round 1: 1 dc into 2nd ch from hook, 1 dc into next 5 ch, 3 dc in end ch, 1 dc in opposite side of each ch (15 sts).

Round 2: 3 ch, *1 dc in next dc, 1 htr in next dc, 1 tr in next 3 dc, 1 htr in next dc,* 1 dc in next 2 dc; rep from * to *, 1 dc in next dc, sl st to next st. Fasten off and weave in ends.

LEAF

MAKING UP

With G and 2.5mm hook, make 10 ch, join with sl st to first ch to form a loop.

Make 9 ch; with top of shoe facing, work 1 dc into the loop at the heel to join, *sl st into 2nd and 3rd ch from hook, 5 ch; with RS of leaf facing, 1 dc into 3-ch sp at end of leaf to join, sl st into 2nd and 3rd ch from hook, 5 ch*; with top of hat facing, 1 dc into edge of brim to join, rep from * to *, join heart with 1 dc into one side of top shaping, rep from * to *; with front of bag facing, 1 dc into 10-ch sp to join, rep from * to *, join cupcake with 1 dc into side of cake, rep from * to *.

Next: 1 ch, join final leaf with 1 dc into 3-ch sp, sl st back along each ch, including the 10 ch forming the loop at the beginning. Fasten off and weave in ends. Pull leaves into shape.

The bracelet size can be altered by crocheting more or fewer stitches between the charms and leaves.

VARIATION:
ALTERNATIVE CUPCAKE CASE

Here is a simple alternative rib pattern for the cake case.

With D and 2.5mm hook, make 5 ch that will form the side seam rather than the lower edge.

Row 1: 1 dc into 2nd ch from hook, 1 dc in next 3 ch, turn (4 sts).

Row 2: 1 ch, 1 dc in back loops only of each dc, turn.

Rep row 2 until work fits snugly around the cake. Finish as given for the cupcake pattern.

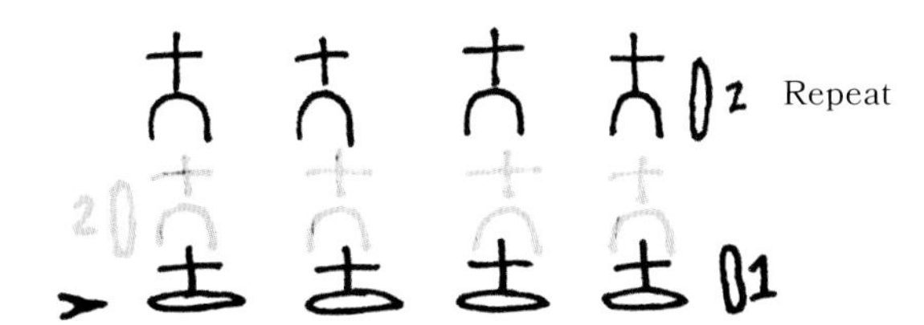

ALTERNATIVE SIMPLE CAKE CASE

VARIATION:
KEYRINGS

Attach a keyring to the charms, using the round-nose pliers to open the small split ring at the end of the chain. Insert the opened ring onto a gap between the stitches and close the ring with the pliers.

HEART RING

This project brings together a classic heart motif with a band, crocheted in an openwork pattern, to make a pretty ring. Gold thread running through the band adds a touch of sparkle.

MATERIALS

- Crochet thread 10 in black and gold metallic (A), pale pink (B)
- 1.25mm (UK3:US8) crochet hook
- Tiny amount of toy stuffing
- Sewing needle

SIZE

Heart measures approximately ⅞in (2.25cm) at widest point and ⅞in (2.25cm) at longest point
Band measures approximately ½in (1.25cm) deep

TENSION

42 sts and 40 rows to 4 in (10cm) over double crochet using 1.25mm hook and A.
Use larger or smaller hook if necessary to obtain correct tension.

NOTE

1 ch at beg of the round does not count as a st throughout.

METHOD

The band is a simple filet design worked in rows and joined at the seam. The heart is made in continuous rounds of double crochet, increasing the stitches to shape it. This ring is crocheted on a larger hook than the other small-scale projects.

KEY

- chain (ch)
- slip stitch (sl st)
- double crochet (dc)
- dc2inc
- half treble (htr)
- treble (tr)

BAND

With 1.25mm hook and A, make 6 ch.

Row 1: 1 tr in first ch to make first space, 4 ch, turn, 1 tr into 6-ch sp, *4 ch, turn, 1 tr into 4-ch sp; rep from * to make the required length to fit around finger loosely, as the finished piece will be tighter.

Row 2: 2 ch (to count as first htr), 1 htr in first 4-ch sp, 2 htr in all but last 6-ch sp, 1 htr in last 6-ch sp, 2 ch, 3 dc in last 6-ch sp.

Row 3: Rotate the piece and, working into opposite side of each space, 2 ch (to count as first htr), 1 htr in first sp, 2 htr in each 4-ch sp to end. Fasten off, leaving a long tail of thread.

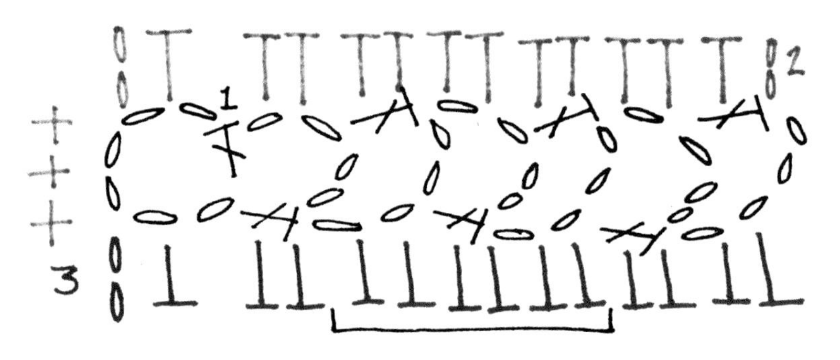

Repeat to required length

BAND

HEART

With 1.25mm hook and B, make a magic loop.

Round 1: 1 ch, 5 dc into loop (5 sts).

Round 2: 1 dc in each st.

Round 3 (inc): (Dc2inc) 5 times. Pull tightly on short end of thread to close loop (10 sts).

Round 4: 1 dc in each st.

Round 5 (inc): (Dc2inc, 1 dc) 5 times (15 sts).

Round 6: 1 dc in each st.

Round 7 (inc): (Dc2inc, 2 dc) 5 times (20 sts).

Round 8: 1 dc in each st.

Shape top

Round 9: 1 dc in next 5 dc, skip next 10 sts, 1 dc in next 5 dc.

Continue on these 10 sts.

Round 10: 1 dc in each st.

Fasten off, leaving a long tail of thread to finish top.

With RS facing, join B with a sl st to the first of the unworked 10 sts. Starting in the same dc as the sl st, work 2 rounds of 1 dc in each st to match first side.

Fasten off, leaving a long tail of thread.

SHAPE TOP ROUND 9

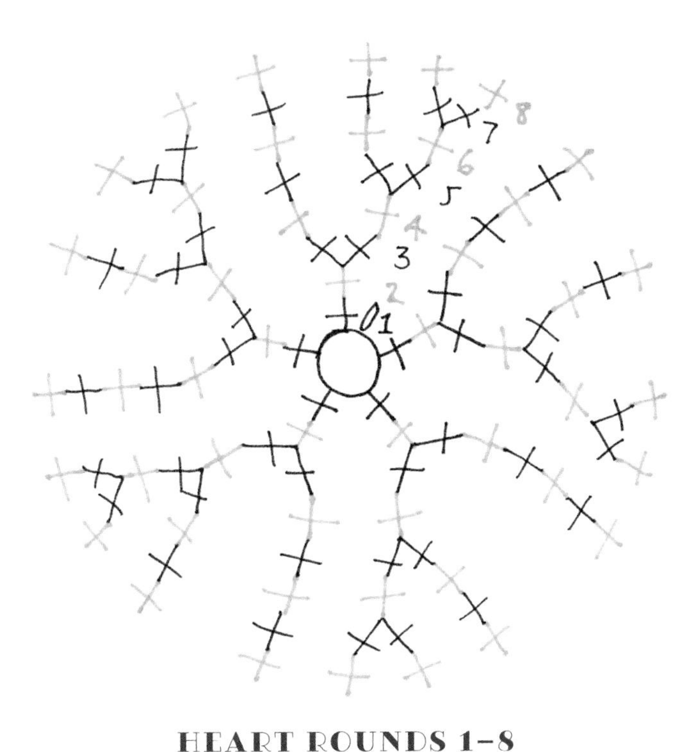

HEART ROUNDS 1–8

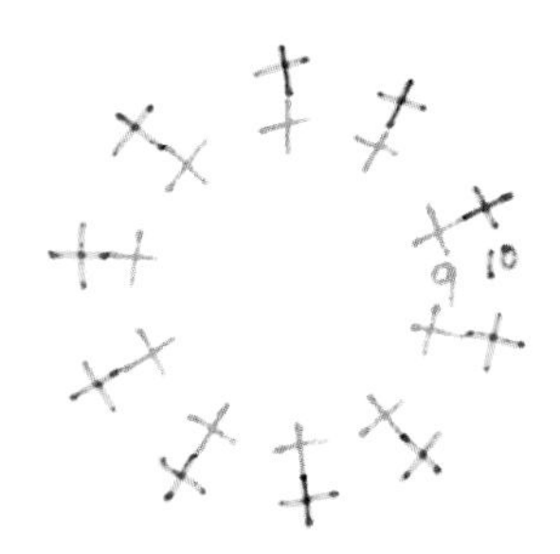

SHAPE TOP ROUND 10

MAKING UP

Stuff the heart firmly. On each side, weave the tail of thread through the last round of stitches. Pull tightly on the thread to close the opening and fasten off. Weave in all the thread ends. Use the tail of thread to join the short ends of the band and stitch the heart over the seam.

TIE PINS, CUFFLINKS & KEYRINGS

BUMBLEBEE

This busy bumblebee is the perfect pin to dress any garment. The tiny, intricately worked wings give the appearance of delicate filigree.

MATERIALS

- Crochet thread 20 in black (A) and yellow (B)
- Embroidery thread in silver, using only 2 strands worked together (C)
- 0.75mm (UK5:US12) crochet hook
- Tiny amount of toy stuffing
- Sewing needle
- PVA glue
- Small paintbrush
- Stickpin and stickpin protector

SIZE

Approximately ⅝in (1.5cm) in length with a wingspan of ⅞in (2.25cm)

TENSION

52 sts and 50 rows to 4in (10cm) over double crochet using 0.75mm hook and A.
Use larger or smaller hook if necessary to obtain correct tension.

NOTE

1 ch and 2 ch at beg of the row/round does not count as a st throughout.

METHOD

The striped body is worked in continuous rounds with shaping to the abdomen and head. The pin is inserted through the back of the body from the inside before stuffing. The lower and upper wings are crocheted in one piece for each side and attached to the finished body after stiffening them with thin layers of PVA glue.

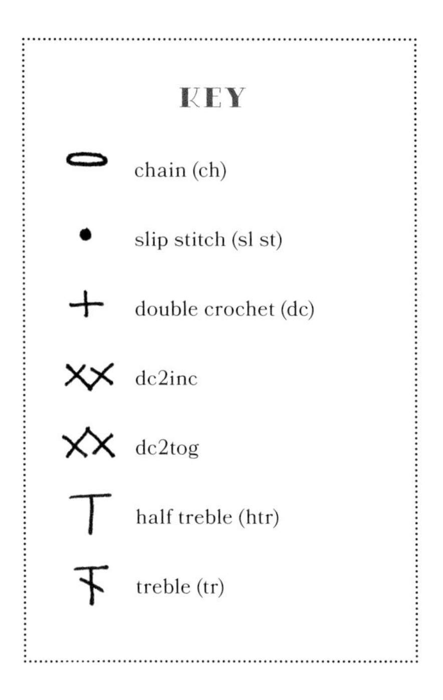

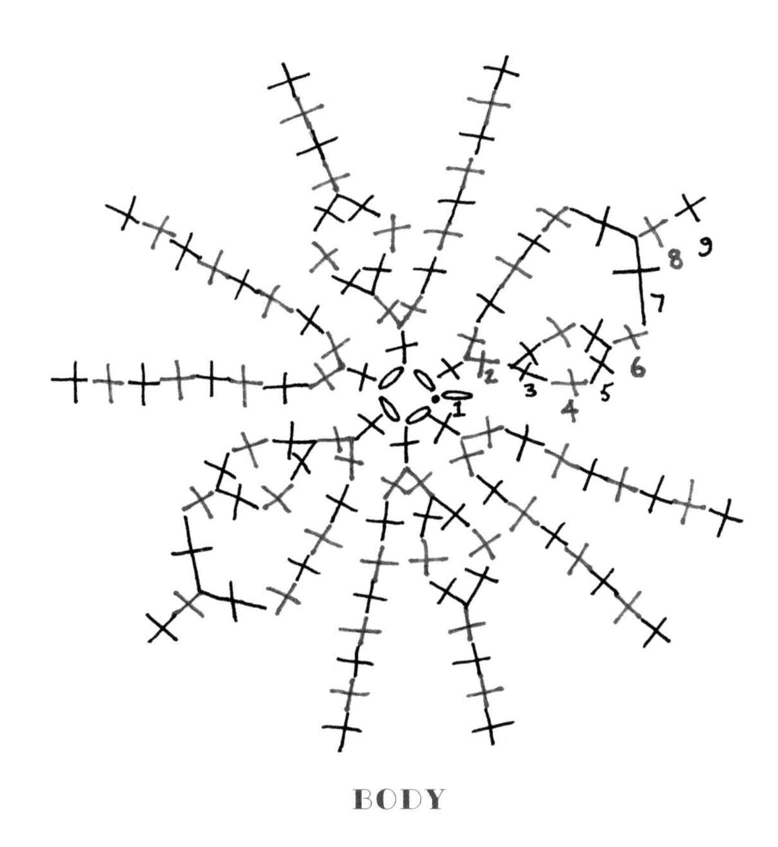

BODY

BODY

With 0.75mm hook and A, make 4 ch and join with sl st to first ch to form a ring.

Round 1: 1 ch, 6 dc into ring. Join B in last dc (6 sts).
Round 2 (inc): (Dc2inc) 6 times with B (12 sts).
Round 3 (inc): With A, (dc2inc, 2 dc) 4 times (16 sts).
Round 4: With B, 1 dc in each st.
Round 5 (dec): With A, (dc2tog, 2 dc) 4 times (12 sts).
Round 6: As round 4.

Shape head

Round 7 (dec): With A, (dc2tog, 4 dc) twice (10 sts).
Rounds 8–9: With A, 1 dc in each st.
Fasten off, leaving a long tail of thread.

Slip the pin through the centre back of the bee from the inside, so it appears between rounds 4 and 5 on the outside of the work. It may need a bit of jiggling to get it in place. Put the protector onto the end of the pin before continuing. Holding the top of the pin so the pad sits flat against the inside, stuff the body firmly, pushing the stuffing in with the end of the crochet hook. Weave the tail of thread through the last round of the head, pull tightly on the thread to close the opening and fasten off.

DOUBLE WING (MAKE 2)

Upper wing

With C and 0.75mm hook, make 6 ch.

Round 1: 1 dc into 2nd ch from hook, 1 dc in next 3 ch, 3 dc in end ch, 1 dc down opposite side of each ch to end (11 sts).

Round 2: 2 ch, 1 dc in next dc, 1 htr in next dc, 1 tr in next dc, 1 htr in next dc, 3 dc in next dc, 1 htr in next dc, 1 tr in next dc, 1 htr in next dc, 1 dc in next dc, sl st into 2-ch sp. Do not fasten off.

Lower wing

Make 8 ch.

Round 1: 1 dc into 2nd ch from hook, 1 dc in next 3 ch, 3 dc in next ch, skip last 2 ch, work 1 dc down opposite side of each ch (11 sts).

Round 2: 2 ch, 1 dc in next dc, 1 htr in next dc, 1 tr in next dc, 1 htr in next dc, 1 dc in next dc, sl st to next st. Fasten off, leaving a long tail of thread and weave in shorter end. Pull into shape and paint the backs of the wings carefully with a little PVA glue. Leave to dry completely.

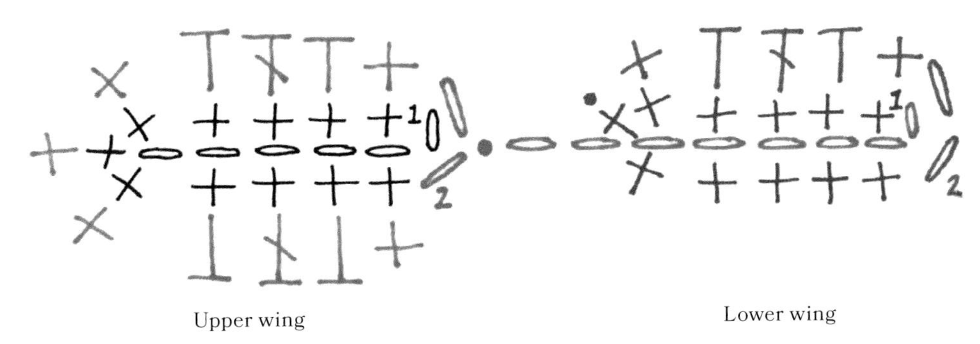

BEE WING

MAKING UP

Position the lower wing so it sits at an angle below the larger upper wing and, using the tail of thread, secure with a couple of stitches before attaching the wings to the side of the bee. Repeat for the second set of wings to mirror the first and stitch to the other side. Paint another coat of glue on the underside of the wings and leave again to dry completely.

VARIATION: NECKLACE

This bee looks lovely as a pendant hanging by a link from a necklace. Make the bee, as above, omitting the stickpin. For the link, make 10 ch using 0.75mm hook and A, join with a sl st to first ch to form a ring. Into the ring work 14 dc, sl st to first dc and fasten off, leaving a long tail of thread. Sew the link to the underside of the bee so the top of it sits hidden behind the head. Leave a gap at the top of the link to thread the chain through.

BUTTON

With 0.75mm hook and A, make 4 ch and join with sl st to first ch to form a ring.

Round 1: 1 ch, 6 dc into ring (6 sts).
Round 2 (inc): (Dc2inc) 6 times (12 sts).
Rounds 3–5: 1 dc in each dc.

Fasten off, leaving a long tail of thread. Stuff the button firmly. Weave the tail of thread through the last round, pull tightly on the thread to close the opening and fasten off.

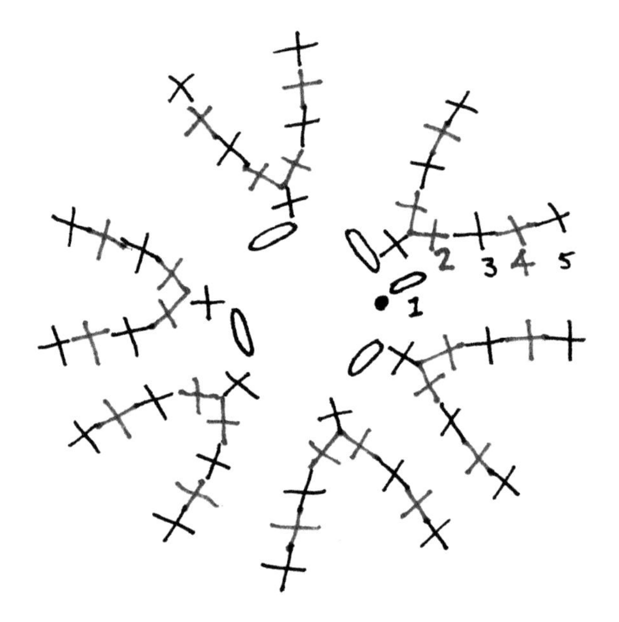

BUTTON

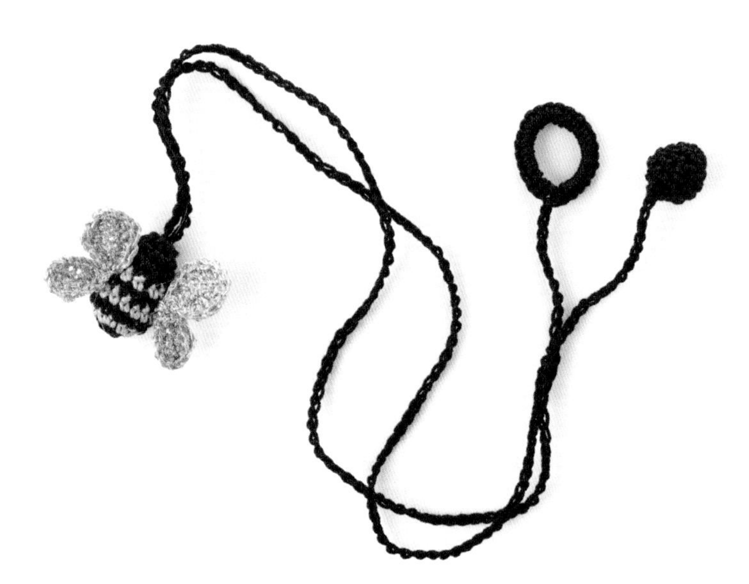

CHAIN AND LOOP

With 0.75mm hook and A, make 16 ch and join with sl st to first ch to form a ring.
1 ch, 24 dc into ring, sl st to first dc.
Next: Work a chain measuring 17in (43cm), or to desired length, allowing an extra ⅝in (1.5cm) for attaching the bee. Fasten off, leaving a tail of thread to stitch the finished chain securely to the gathered end of the button. Fold the chain in the middle to form a loop and thread it through the link, using a crochet hook to catch it and draw it through. Pass the ends of the necklace through the looped chain. Pull on the ends to tighten the loop.

CHAIN AND LOOP

VARIATION: THREADS

The look of the finished bee can be transformed simply by changing the threads. Experiment with a fine cotton or linen for the wings. Gold-coloured machine embroidery thread can be used together with the yellow for the stripes, which will catch the light for extra sparkle.

TRIANGLE & HEART

These triangular-shaped cufflinks are attached to the cuffs by a small bead on one and a heart on the other, making them a perfect creative gift.

MATERIALS

- Crochet thread 20 in black (A) and red (B)
- 0.75mm (UK5:US12) crochet hook
- Tiny amount of toy stuffing
- Sewing needle

For the pin variation:

- Stickpin and stickpin protector

SIZE

The triangles and heart measure approximately ⅝in (1.5cm) x ⅝in (1.5cm)
The bead is approximately ⅝in (1.5cm) long

TENSION

52 sts and 50 rows to 4in (10cm) over double crochet using 0.75mm hook and A.
Use larger or smaller hook if necessary to obtain correct tension.

NOTE

1 ch at beg of the round does not count as a st throughout.

METHOD

The triangles, heart and bead are worked in continuous rounds of double crochet. The triangles are padded out with a little toy stuffing and the top edges are joined by slip stitching the stitches together. A short foundation chain in doubled thread links the two pieces of each cufflink.

KEY

- chain (ch)
- slip stitch (sl st)
- double crochet (dc)
- dc2inc
- slip stitch together back loops on each side to join

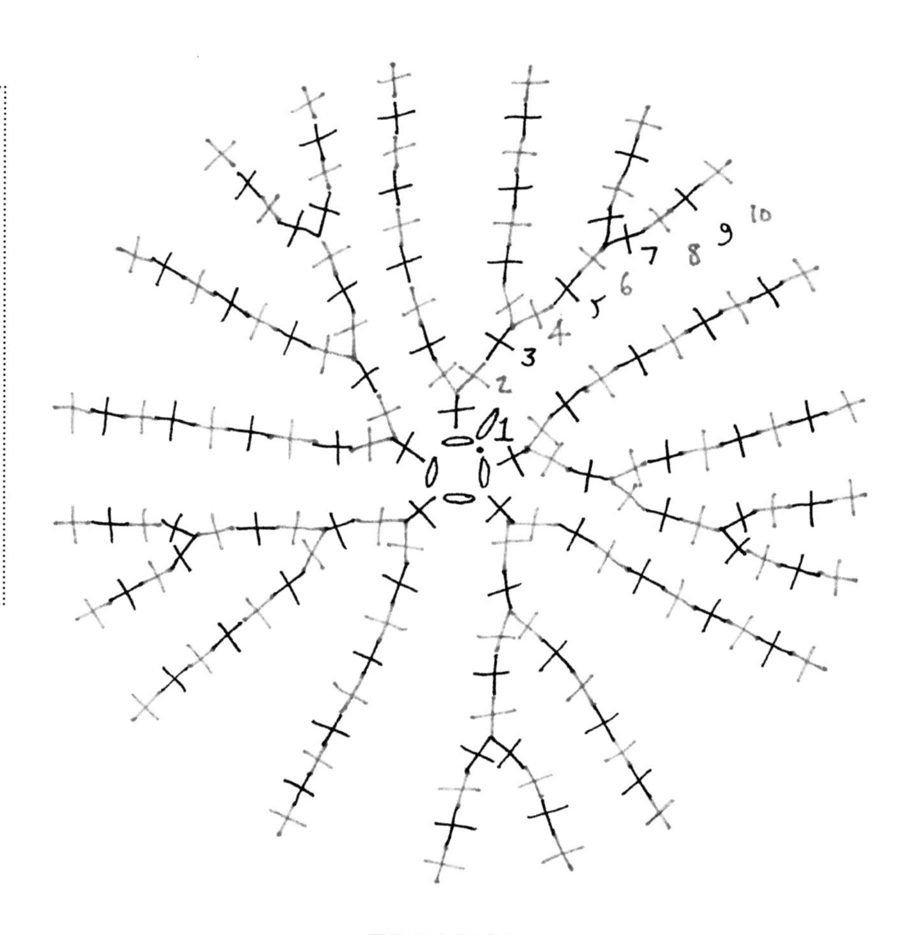

TRIANGLE

TRIANGLE (MAKE 2)

With 0.75mm hook and A, make 4 ch and join with a sl st to first ch to form a ring.

Round 1: 1 ch, 5 dc into ring (5 sts).

Round 2 (inc): (Dc2inc) 5 times (10 sts).

Round 3: 1 dc in each st.

Round 4 (inc): (Dc2inc, 1 dc) 5 times (15 sts).

Rounds 5–6: 1 dc in each st.

Round 7 (inc): (Dc2inc, 2 dc) 5 times (20 sts).

Rounds 8–10: 1 dc in each st.

This will form a cone shape. Do not fasten off. Stuff the shape, but do not over stuff.

Next: Sl st together the back loops of the next 10 sts on each side of the opening to join and form the triangle. Fasten off and weave in ends.

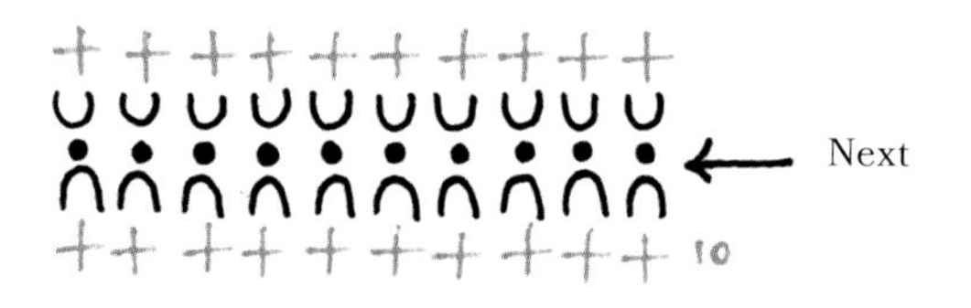

TRIANGLE

HEART

With 0.75mm hook and B, make 4 ch and join with a sl st to first ch to form a ring.

Round 1: 1 ch, 6 dc into ring (6 sts).

Round 2 (inc): (Dc2inc) 6 times (12 sts).

Rounds 3–4: 1 dc in each st.

Round 5 (inc): (Dc2inc, 2 dc) 4 times (16 sts).

Rounds 6–7: 1 dc in each st.

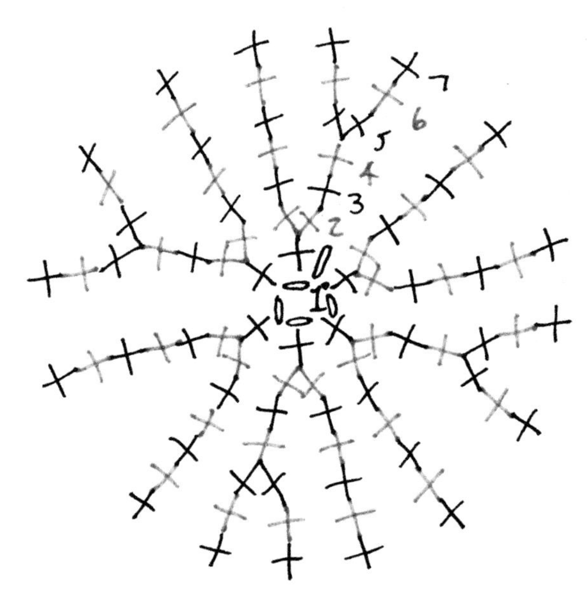

HEART ROUNDS 1–7

Shape top

Round 8: 1 dc in next 4 dc, skip next 8 sts, 1 dc in next 4 dc.

Continue on these 8 sts.

Rounds 9–10: 1 dc in each st.

Fasten off, leaving a long tail of thread to finish top.

With RS facing, join B with a sl st to the first of the unworked 8 sts. Starting in the same dc as the sl st, work 3 rounds of 1 dc in each st to match first side. Fasten off, leaving a long tail of thread.

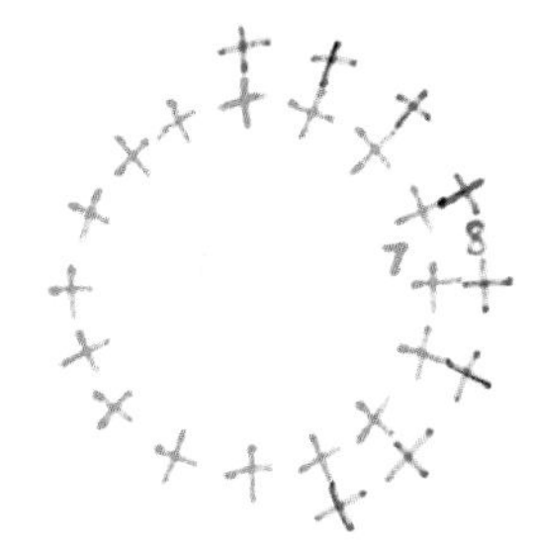

SHAPE TOP ROUND 8

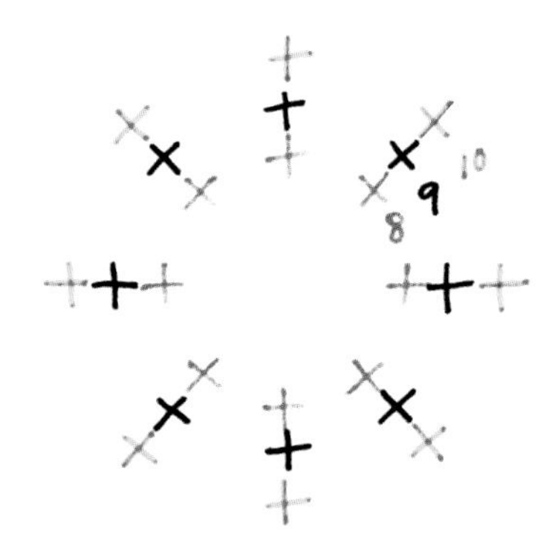

SHAPE TOP ROUNDS 9–10

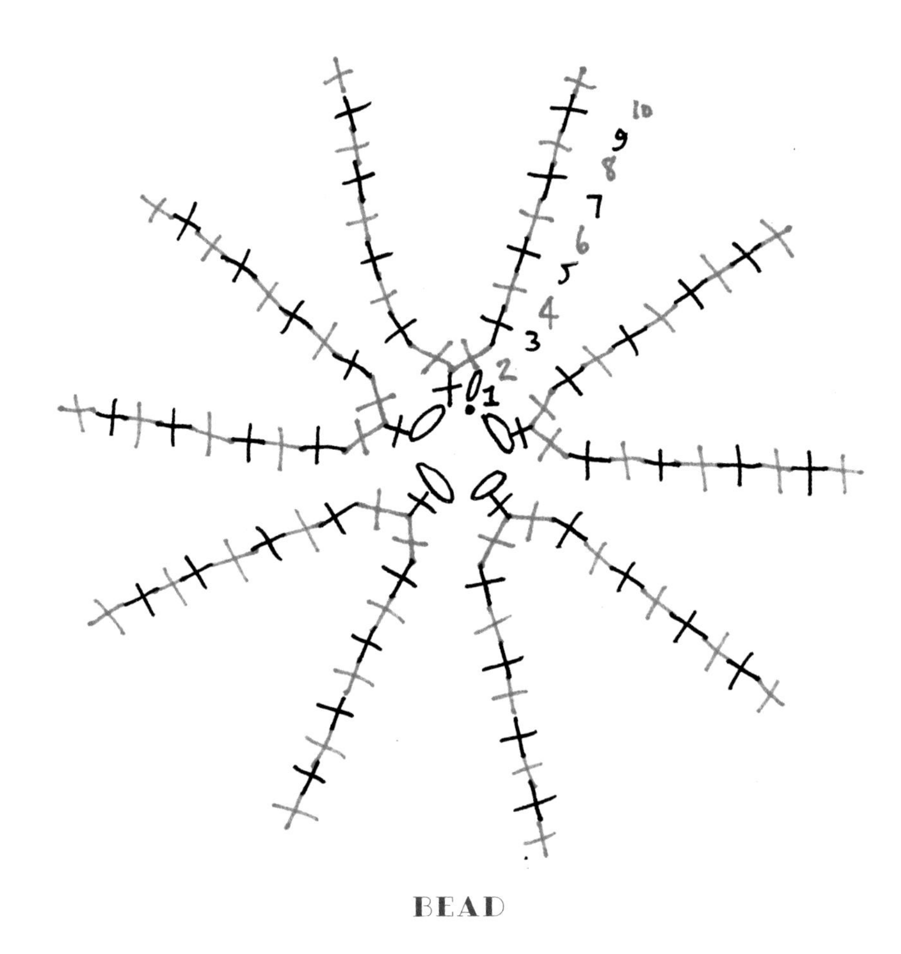

BEAD

BEAD

With 0.75mm hook and A, make 4 ch and join with a sl st to form a ring.

Round 1: 1 ch, 5 dc into ring (5 sts).

Round 2 (inc): (Dc2inc) 5 times, (10 sts).

Rounds 3–10: 1 dc in each st. The work tends to curl inside out on the first few rounds, so use the end of the crochet hook to help turn the RS out on the 3rd or 4th round.

Fasten off, leaving a long tail of thread.

MAKING UP

Stuff the bead firmly, using the other end of the crochet hook to push the stuffing down. Weave the tail of thread through the last round of stitches. Pull tightly on the thread to close the opening and fasten off. Stuff the heart, but not too firmly as it may not fit through the buttonhole if it is over-stuffed. Finish the open ends as for the bead.

LINK

With 0.75mm hook and A doubled, work 1 dc into the middle of the length of the bead, 7 ch, fasten off, leaving a long tail of thread to stitch the link to the triangle. Weave in remaining ends. Repeat for the other cufflink, working the dc into the centre of the back of the heart.

LINK (USE THREAD DOUBLED)

VARIATION: TIE PIN

Follow the instructions to make the heart. After completing rounds 8–10 to shape the first side of the top of the heart, insert the pin through the back of the heart, between rounds 6 and 7. Put the protector on to the end of the pin before continuing. After completing the other side of the top shaping, stuff the heart, ensuring the flat pad of the pin is pressed against the inside. Gather and close the top edges as for the cufflink.

MOD TARGETS

Capturing the iconic imagery of youth and rebellion in 1960s Britain, these target cufflinks are an impressive gift that can easily be adapted to make a tie pin for the matching set.

MATERIALS

- Crochet thread 20 in red (A), white (B) and blue (C)
- 0.75mm (UK5:US12) crochet hook
- Tiny amount of toy stuffing
- Sewing needle

For target pin variation:

- Flat-plated pin and clutch back

For keyring variation:

- 4ply yarn in red (A), white (B) and blue (C)
- 2.5mm (UK12:US-) crochet hook
- Keyring
- Round-nose pliers

SIZE

Target measures approximately
5⁄8in (1.5cm) in diameter
Bead measures approximately
3⁄4in (1.75cm) long

> **NOTE**
> **1 ch at beg of the round does not count as a st throughout.**

TENSION

52 sts and 50 rows to 4in (10cm) over double crochet using 0.75mm hook and A.
Use larger or smaller hook if necessary to obtain correct tension.

METHOD

The main pieces are worked in continuous rounds of double crochet, joining in the colours and increasing the stitches to form the front of the target design. The stitches are then decreased to shape the back and continued in blue thread. The beads are made separately and the pieces joined with a length of chain stitches using doubled thread.

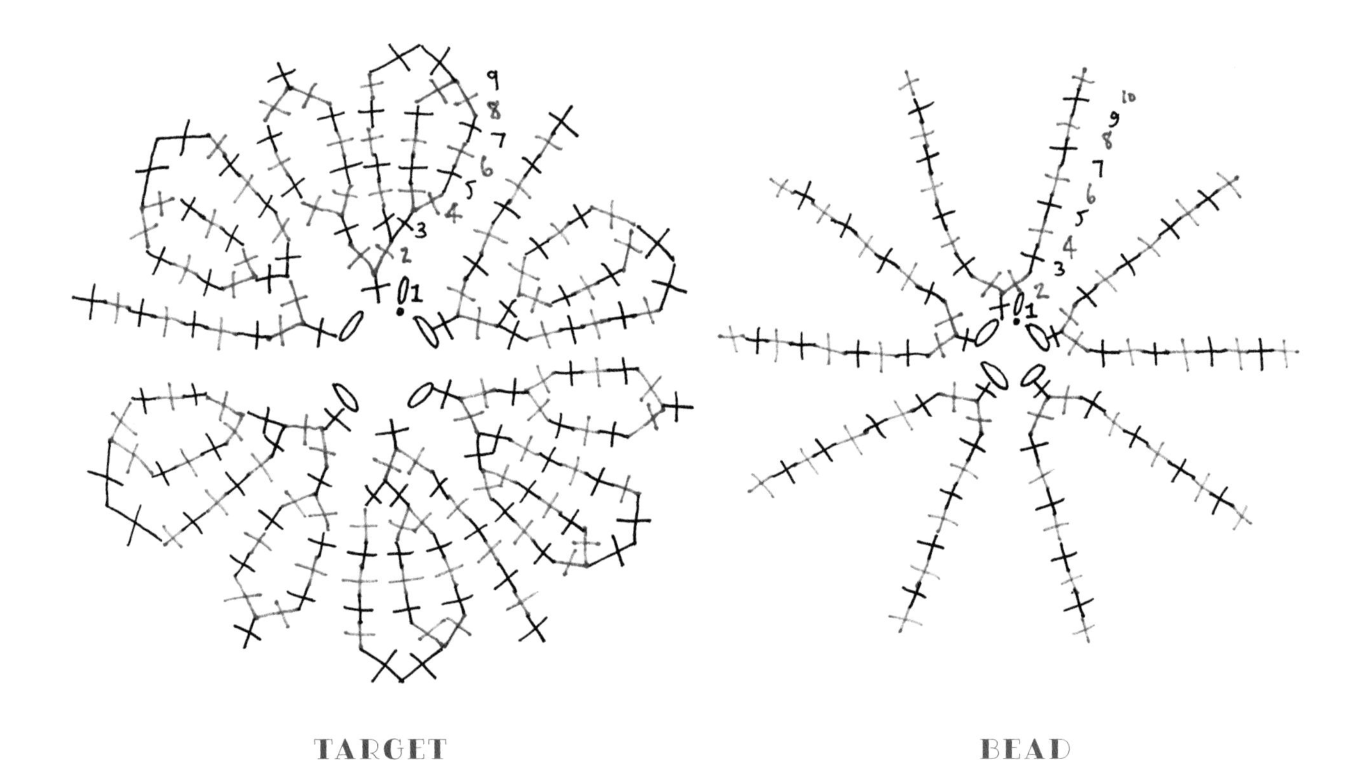

TARGET (MAKE 2)

With 0.75mm hook and A, leaving a long tail of thread at the beginning, make 4 ch and join with a sl st to first ch to form a ring.

Round 1: 1 ch, 6 dc into ring, sl st to first dc with B (6 sts).

Round 2 (inc): With B, (dc2inc) 6 times (12 sts)

Round 3 (inc): (Dc2inc, 1 dc) 6 times, sl st to first dc with C (18 sts).

Round 4 (inc): With C, (dc2inc, 1 dc) 9 times (27 sts).

Rounds 5–7: 1 dc in each st.

Round 8 (dec): (Dc2tog, 1 dc) 9 times (18 sts).

Round 9 (dec): (Dc2tog, 1 dc) 6 times (12 sts).

Fasten off, leaving a long tail of C.

BEAD (MAKE 2)

With 0.75mm hook and C, make 4 ch and join with a sl st to form a ring.

Round 1: 1 ch, 5 dc into ring (5 sts).

Round 2 (inc): (Dc2inc) 5 times, (10 sts).

Rounds 3–10: 1 dc in each st.

Fasten off, leaving long length of thread.

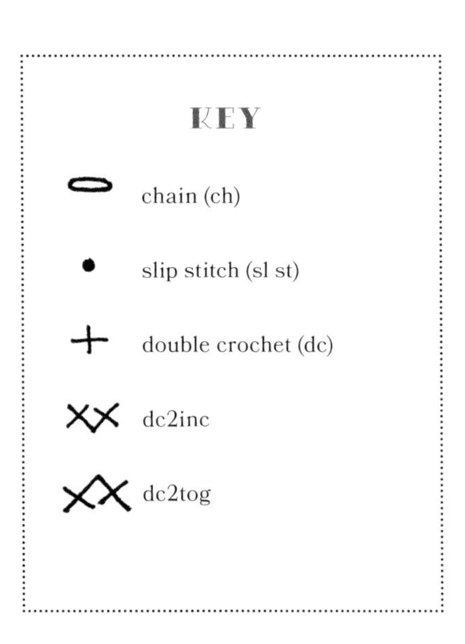

MAKING UP

Stuff the target. With the tail of A left at the beginning, work a few stitches from the centre through the stuffing and back again to flatten the shape. Thread the tail of C through the last round, pull tightly on the thread to close the opening and fasten off.

Stuff the bead firmly. Weave the tail of thread through the last round, pull tightly on the thread to close the opening and fasten off. Weave in all the ends.

LINK

With 0.75mm hook and C doubled, work 1 dc into the middle of the length of the bead, 7 ch, fasten off, leaving a long tail of thread to stitch the link to the target. Weave in remaining ends.

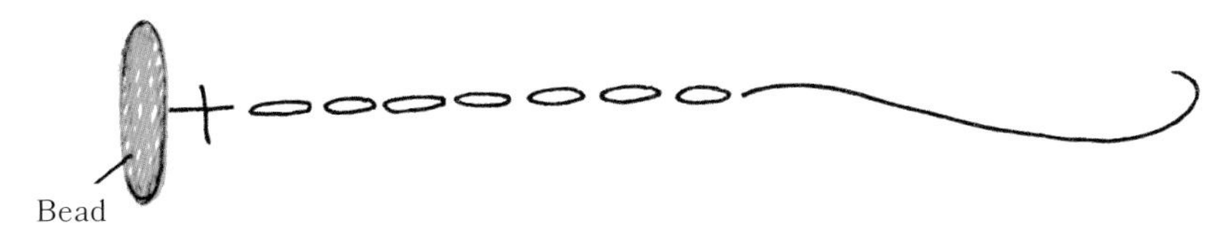

LINK (USE THREAD DOUBLED)

VARIATION: PIN

Work as for target from rounds 1 to 6, and rounds 8 to 9.
Stuff the shape as for cufflinks, inserting a flat-plated pin before gathering up the last round of stitches to close. Add a clutch back to the pin to secure it to the wearer's clothing.

VARIATION: KEYRING

With 2.5mm hook and A, leaving a long length of yarn at the beginning, make a magic loop.
Making one target, following rounds 1 to 9 of the target pattern, pulling tightly on the long end left at the beginning of A to close the ring before finishing off, as for the target. Attach the keyring to the side of the target, using the pliers to open the small split ring at the end of the chain. Insert the opened ring onto a gap between the stitches and close the ring with the pliers.

FANTAIL DOVE

These flighty fantailed doves form a confetti group of pretty keyrings – evocative of a magician's star turn, conjuring birds from his top hat that flit to the heights of the circus tent.

MATERIALS

- 4ply yarn in any shade (A)
- Embroidery threads or oddments of yarn in black and yellow or metallic gold
- 2.5mm (UK12:US-) crochet hook
- Small amount of toy stuffing
- Blunt-ended yarn needle
- Keyring
- Round-nose pliers

For brooch variation:
1in (2.5cm) brooch bar

SIZE

Approximately 2in (5cm) from head to tail end (excluding fantail)

TENSION

26 sts and 26 rows to 4in (10cm) over double crochet using 2.5mm hook and A.
Use larger or smaller hook if necessary to obtain correct tension.

METHOD

The body is worked in continuous rounds of double crochet, starting from the base and finishing at the back of the bird. It is then folded, stuffed and the edges are joined by slip stitching the last round of stitches together, leaving one end open for a few more rounds of double crochet to shape the head. The wings and tail are made separately and attached to the stuffed body. The dove is finished with embroidered features and a keyring.

NOTE

1 ch at beg of the row/round does not count as a st throughout.

BODY

With 2.5mm hook and A, make 4 ch and join with a sl st to the first ch to form a ring.

Round 1: 1 ch, 5 dc into ring (5 sts).

Round 2 (inc): (Dc2inc) 5 times (10 sts).

Round 3: 1 dc in each st.

Round 4 (inc): (Dc2inc) 10 times (20 sts).

Round 5: 1 dc in each st.

Round 6 (inc): (Dc2inc, 1 dc) 10 times (30 sts).

Round 7: Fold piece and sl st together the back loops of the next 10 sts on each side to join the back of the dove, 1 dc into each of the remaining 10 sts to form the start of the head.

BODY ROUNDS 1–6

Shape head

Rounds 8–9: 1 dc into each st. Fasten off, leaving a long tail of yarn. Stuff the bird. Thread the tail of yarn through the last round of stitches, pull tightly on the yarn to close the opening and fasten off. With A, sew a row of stitches below the start of the head shaping and pull on the yarn, but not to tightly, to indicate the neck. Fasten off.

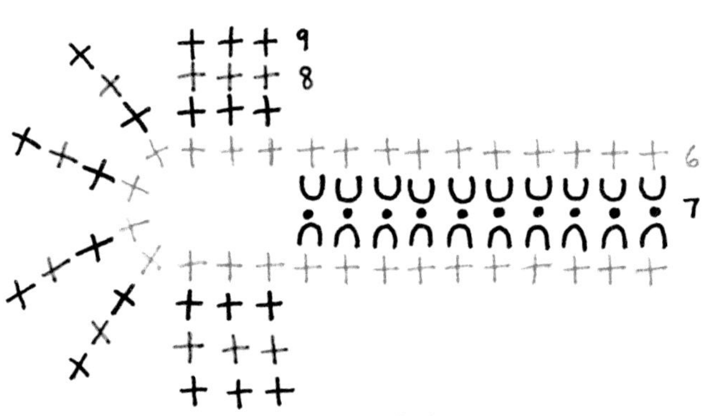

BODY ROUNDS 7–9

KEY

- chain (ch)
- slip stitch (sl st)
- double crochet (dc)
- dc2inc
- half treble (htr)
- treble (tr)
- tr2inc
- slip stitch together back loops on each side to join

WING (MAKE 2)

With 2.5mm hook and A, make 11 ch.

Row 1 (RS): 1 dc in 2nd ch from hook, *1 htr in next ch, 1 tr in next 6 ch, 1 htr in next ch*, 2 dc in end ch; rep from * to * down opposite side of ch, 1 dc in next ch (20 sts).

Do not fasten off.

Join edges

Row 2: Fold the wing lengthways with WS together and sl st together the back loops of the next 10 sts on each side at the same time to join.

Fasten off, leaving a long tail of yarn to sew the wings to the body.

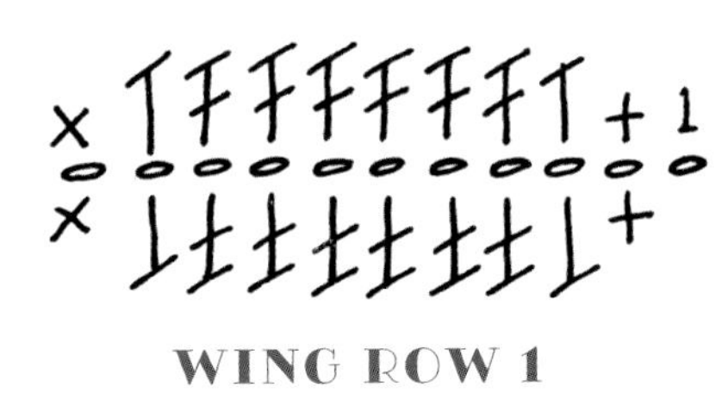

WING ROW 1

WING ROW 2

FANTAIL

With 2.5mm hook and A, leaving a long tail of yarn at the beginning, make 7 ch.

Row 1 (WS): 1 dc into 2nd ch from hook, 1 dc into next 5 ch, turn (6 sts).

Row 2 (RS) (inc): 3 ch (counts as first tr), 1 tr in same st as 3 ch, (tr2inc) 5 times, turn (12 sts).

Row 3 (inc): 3 ch (counts as first tr), 1 tr in same st as 3 ch, (tr2inc) 11 times, turn (24 sts).

Row 4: 1 ch, 1 dc in next 24 sts.

Fasten off, leaving a long tail of yarn at the end. Weave the tail of yarn through the foundation chain at the narrow end of the fantail, gather up and stitch to the end of the body with the RS facing towards the head. The tail will curl naturally.

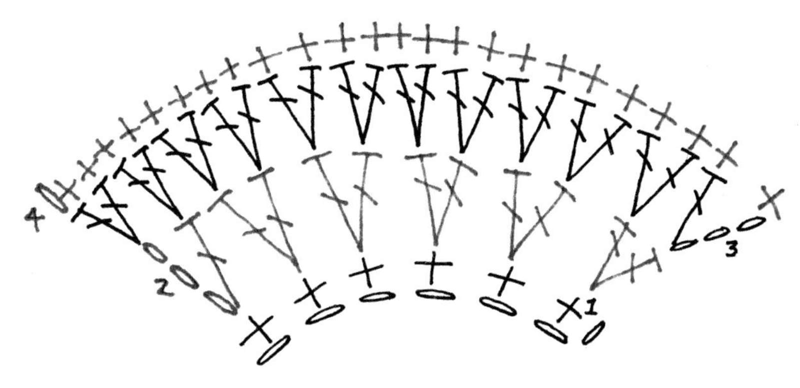

FANTAIL

MAKING UP

With the curved, folded edges positioned at the top, sew the wings to the body. Using oddments of black and gold, or yellow, embroider the eyes and beak. Attach the keyring to the dove's back, using the pliers to open the small split ring at the end of the chain. Insert the opened ring onto a gap between the stitches and close the ring with the pliers.

VARIATION: BROOCH

Attach a brooch bar to the base of the dove to wear it as a brooch. Sew through each hole on both sides, or around the bar if there are no holes.

RESOURCES

SUPPLIERS

YARN

Drops Design
garnstudio.com

King Cole Ltd
kingcole.co.uk

LoveCrafts Group Ltd
lovecrafts.com

Purl Soho
purlsoho.com

Rowan
knitrowan.com

Scheepjes
scheepjes.com

Sirdar Spinning Ltd
sirdar.com

The Stitchery
the-stitchery.co.uk

Stylecraft
stylecraft-yarns.co.uk

Wool Warehouse
woolwarehouse.co.uk

CROCHET HOOKS

LoveCrafts Group Ltd
see under Yarn

Purl Soho
See under Yarn

The Stitchery
See under Yarn

Wool Warehouse
See under Yarn

HABERDASHERY

MacCulloch & Wallis
macculloch-wallis.co.uk

Ray Stitch
raystitch.co.uk

The Stitchery
See under Yarn

BEADS, FINDINGS & JEWELLERY TOOLS

Beads Unlimited
beadsunlimited.co.uk

The Bead Shop
mailorder-beads.co.uk

Kernowcraft Rocks & Gems Ltd
kernowcraft.com

BOOKS

Vintage needlework books are an amazing source of historical reference. Put the titles into your search engine to find booksellers or digital libraries that stock them.

The Lady's Crochet Book by Elvina Mary Corbould (1878)

Encyclopedia of Needlework by Thérèse de Dillmont (1884)

The Complete Book of Crochet by Elizabeth L. Mathieson (1946)

A Complete Guide to Crochet, ed. Pam Dawson (1981)

ABBREVIATIONS

ch	chain
cm	centimetre(s)
dc	double crochet
dc2inc	work 2 double crochet stitches into the next stitch to increase
dc2tog	work 2 double crochet stitches together to decrease
dec	decrease
dtr	double treble
dtr2inc	work 2 double treble stitches into the next stitch to increase
dtr3inc	work 3 double treble stitches into the next stitch to increase
htr	half treble
htr2inc	work 2 half treble stitches into the next stitch to increase
in	inch(es)
inc	increase
m	metre(s)
mm	millimetre(s)
rep	repeat
RS	right side
sl st	slip stitch
sp	space
st(s)	stitch(es)
tog t	ogether
tr	treble
tr2inc	work 2 half treble stitches into the next stitch to increase
tr3tog	work 3 treble stitches together to decrease
trtr	triple treble
WS	wrong side
yd	yard(s)
yrh	yarn round hook

CONVERSIONS

UK/US CROCHET TERMS

UK	US
Double crochet	single crochet
Half treble	half double crochet
Treble	double crochet
Double treble	triple crochet
Triple treble	double triple crochet

Note: this book uses UK crochet terms

ABOUT THE AUTHOR

Vanessa Mooncie spent many happy hours as a child sitting with her mother and grandmother learning to knit and crochet. She went on to study fashion and textile design and became an illustrator, and a designer for children's wear and interiors.

She lives with her husband in a rural village in the south of England. Vanessa has written several books for GMC Publications, including *Crocheted Cats, Crocheted Bees, Bugs and Butterflies, Animal Heads, Crocheted Birds* and *The Gentleman's Wardrobe*. She has also written projects for various craft magazines and yarn companies.

ACKNOWLEDGEMENTS

I was very excited when I was told my first book, *Crocheted Accessories*, was going to be republished with a brand new look! Thank you very much Jonathan Bailey, Sara Harper and all at GMC. Thank you to Anna Stevens and Andrew Perris for the beautiful styling and photography. Thank you to my wonderful, supportive husband, children and grandchildren, who encourage and inspire me. I dedicate this book to Brenda and Eva, my mother and grandmother, who taught me to crochet and sparked my creative passion.

INDEX

First published 2024 by Guild of Master Craftsman Publications Ltd, Castle Place, 166 High Street, Lewes, East Sussex BN7 1XU, UK

ISBN 978-1-78494-696-8

A catalogue record for this book is available from the British Library.

Publisher Jonathan Bailey
Production Jim Bulley
Senior Project Editor Sara Harper
Design Manager Robin Shields
Photographer Andrew Perris
Stylist Anna Stevens
Illustrations Vanessa Mooncie

Colour origination by GMC Reprographics
Printed and bound in China

To order a book, contact:
GMC Publications Ltd
Castle Place, 166 High Street, Lewes,
East Sussex, BN7 1XU
United Kingdom
Tel: +44 (0)1273 488005
www.gmcbooks.com